the Unnamed Zookeeper

Stories to Inspire the Best You

[signature: Samantha]

[signature: Jennie Senapatiratne]

JENNIE SENAPATIRATNE

featuring

Samantha Rose

The Unnamed Zookeeper: Stories to inspire the best you
Copyright © 2021, Jennie Senapatiratne

To my Grandma Ostlund

*She was always my cheerleader
and an example of a real-life faith hero!*

Table of Contents

Preface

I started this book on a journey to see the women of the Bible as more than their stories. I wanted to view their circumstances through the lenses of their cultures, their different strengths and weaknesses, and their worries. I wanted to put myself in their place without knowing the ending God had for them.

I wanted to approach their stories just as I do my life. I don't know the end of my story, let alone what we're eating for dinner. The people in the Bible only had their pasts and the present—what was going on in front of them at that very moment in time—to go on. Their unwavering trust in God during some very shaky circumstances shows me that I can trust God with my out of control life.

As we explore Bible stories you thought you knew, and maybe even a few new ones, I want you to set aside the ending. Let go of what you've learned about these people in the past. Step into their stories, imagining that you're the one living in that time period.

You're in the land of no pavement, no electricity, and no Bible. You are fully depending on God.

Let their stories speak to you. Read through them slowly, and write down your thoughts and dreams as you apply the lessons to your own life. Don't be afraid to ask God for big things. Let the journeys of these women rejuvenate a dream you set aside. Laugh or cry with them as they journey through a situation that reminds you of your current place in life.

But above all, see and know that you are not alone. God placed these women in the Bible to show us that we are not the only ones who struggle. God sees you where you are today. He has a plan to give you hope and a future.

How would things change for us if we viewed our lives through that lens? If we truly had nothing but hope that God is for us. He will get us through. Let's open our hearts and minds as we start to relearn the women of the Bible.

We all have a story. Stories full of joy, disappointment, and adventure. Take time to explore in the next chapters what God can do through and for you, and reflect on how much he loves you.

one

Risk-Taker

Ruth 2-4

Ruth has always fascinated me; she makes all mother-in-law jokes null and void. One of the only women in the Bible with a book named after her, her story takes place during the time of the judges. Ruth enters the story after Naomi loses her husband. Ruth marries Naomi's son, Mahlon, and has 10 blissful years with him.

We are not told how Mahlon dies or how Ruth's brother-in-law dies. If they died together, weeks or months apart. We just know of their deaths and the lack of any heirs. Ruth was without a husband and her mother-in-law decides to go home. Ruth has lived her whole life in Moab, though likely in her late 20s; she has known nothing different. Despite the fear of the unknown, she packs up and follows Naomi.

At some point in the journey, Naomi turns to her daughters-in-law and tells them to go back to their homes. Find their moms and start over again. Orpah turns around and goes home. Ruth says something we all hold to be great.

"I will go with you, your home will be my home and your God my God."

I just have to say it. *Wow*. I am not sure that would have been my response.

I have spent most of life with the image of Ruth as a demur young lady who followed all the rules. Ruth simply goes with the flow, not wanting her mother-in-law to be alone. She unassumingly takes responsibility on her shoulders. But with this statement we really ought to picture the image of a woman in a plane, watching as her mother-in-law falls through the sky. Before she pulls her shoot, Ruth jumps out of the plane yelling, "I will follow you, your God is my God now!"

The risk Ruth takes to follow Naomi is high. Her sister-in-law takes the safe way out. Orpah stayed in the plane and presumably made it comfortably back to safety, where she could only imagine the adventures Ruth and Naomi would have. Ruth jumps in with both feet.

She could be worried about going home to her mom and starting over, she could be under some kind of obligation to Naomi to take care of her, or she could be looking for adventure…we aren't given those details. But I look at the rest of her story and see that she was a risk taker who believed in Naomi's God. Her God was their provider. Ruth must have understood and known God on a deeper level than just knowing him to be Naomi's God.

I am not sure that I could leave the U.S. and go to another country, one with different customs and religions, if it was someone else's idea. Now, if it were *my* idea, and God called me personally, I would start packing! I would be so excited that I would be shouting from the rooftops about the dream that God had given me to follow. In Ruth's life, losing her husband and moving were not in her plan, yet she stood in faith that it was God's plan.

Ruth has always been the person I thought I acted most like in the Bible. She followed the rules, followed without question, and seemed submissive. I am not particularly proud of this fact as I have always wanted to be a risk taker, a woman who makes her own rules. I have discovered that I hate the maintenance of life. I like starting new things and if I finish them, great, but if I have to continue to finish them day after day, they're not my thing. Like dishes or laundry. I am not good at either. (Can I get an amen?) Making the bed is only done in my house because it is important to my husband; it seems silly to me. Knowing this about me, you'll see why I have not been proud of myself acting like Ruth, riding the waves someone else makes, instead of making my own.

We all want to make a difference, and the difference we want to make looks different to each of us. How do you want to make a difference? I want people to take time and go beyond the Bible stories to see the women in the Bible in a new way. Take time to write down a few of your ideas. God has given each person a unique look at the world. What makes your thoughts stand out?

In this short, four-chapter book of Ruth, we continue to follow Ruth's adventure. Once I considered all she did, I became excited to be like her. She went into a field and tried to provide for herself and her mother-in-law. Finally, a super saver like me! I know it was tradition, but let's give her credit for taking care of her family by clipping coupons, I mean, clipping grain. She did not sit back and wait for the Rescuer to help them. She was a woman of action and showed her work ethic. She was noticed and highly praised. Ruth was not being a wallflower in those fields, she stepped into them with faith in her heart.

Ruth not only provides food for herself and Naomi, but she gains favor from Boaz, the landlord of those fields. Naomi gives Ruth instructions to lay at Boaz's feet. This part of her story has always confused me. Let me stop here, as many have said it was not his feet she uncovered. In my humble opinion, whatever she uncovered, in a dark barn full of other workers, was bold! So for our purposes, we're going to stick with feet.

Can you imagine yourself in this scenario? This scene is a flashback to my youth. I was a boy crazy teen girl; I liked a different boy at every camp, until I met my husband. At camps there was always talk about sneaking out at night to go chat with campers of the opposite sex. I did not, of course, for fear of running into a counselor or into the wrong boy's cabin. So here is young Ruth, being told to go into Boaz's cabin and stay there until he notices. Seems like a good plan if you want to get kicked out of camp, or worse, get a bad reputation. What if she uncovered the wrong guy in the dark?? EEK!

Ruth impresses me with her calmness throughout this process. There is no crying out to God, "Please use someone else!" or laying down of a fleece (see Judges 6) before she did this crazy scheme. Ruth goes in to Boaz's cabin and does exactly what Naomi says. Then Boaz says leave before anyone sees you and I will see if I can marry you. WHAT?! Sorry, she just did this risky thing to say "dude marry me" and he replies "we will see." I would not have been happy. But Ruth trusts, and becomes part of the lineage of Jesus!

Ruth's boldness was guided by godly advice and by her faith that God had a plan.

I have been praying for adventure for years…remember, I hate maintenance. *Lord, give me something different to do for you.* But when choices come my way, I seem to choose the easy way. I guess I am a flawed person, and my faith is easily shaken. But what if one day, we listened to and acted on God's calling to encourage to the person behind us in church? What if you shared your crazy dream with a friend? What if you packed up your home to follow God's call on your life?

What adventure is God calling you to? How do you know if it is God? Right?! I so often think that there is no way that God needs *me* to be the one to lay down at the feet of someone to work a miracle. The truth is that God does not *need* me, but rather, He is *giving* me the opportunity.

An opportunity is a set of circumstances that makes it possible to do something. Take this as a cue to look around and ask God what opportunities He may have for you. Maybe not for life, maybe just a couple of weeks or a month or two. We know that God has a plan if we ask.

Will you ask?

Reflection Verse

The LORD directs the steps of the godly.
He delights in every detail of their lives.

Psalm 37:23 NLT

So we can say with confidence, "The Lord is my helper, so I will have no fear. What can mere people do to me?"

Hebrews 13:6 NLT

two

Hidden in Plain Sight

John 4:4-28

Do you want to see the true love of the Father? There are few stories in which it is so poignantly shown than in the story of Jesus' interaction with a woman who was looked down on for many reasons.

This woman, we do not know her name. But we are going to call her Jill. Jack and Jill went up the hill to get a pail of water...

Jill was not a Jewish woman; she was a Samaritan. A Samaritan was half Jewish and half Gentile. Not accepted by either group, they lived in shame together, in an area called Samaria. They had their own place of worship and they followed the first five books of the Bible. And while I always thought they were shunned because of their religious beliefs, the truth is that they were not full Jews, and were shunned because of their race.

Jesus, being a man who never ran from conflict or uncomfortable situations, went through the area of Samaria. Jill was quite the opposite. She avoided conflict and uncomfortable situations at ALL costs. Getting water at the well in the afternoon heat was a huge price to pay just to avoid the uncomfortable looks and whispers from others.

When I was a kid, my mom made me and my siblings try everything on our plate. EEK! Beets, the devil in disguise, were one of my mom's favorite veggies. Oh how my mom loved beets. I tried everything I could think of to make them taste worthy of swallowing, but there was never enough butter or even sugar to make those little piles of purple torture edible. Yet every time they made it to my plate, I had to eat one or two of them. I did everything I could to avoid them. I hid them, smashed them, tried to feed them to my brother. But nothing ever worked because my mom was a hawk.

Avoiding things in life takes lots of energy. I spent more time trying to avoid beets than it would have taken to quickly swallow one with my nose plugged. And most of the time, avoiding things just makes the actual thing you're avoiding worse. When you avoid things, your focus is on the thing you are trying to avoid. Funny, we focus on a thing we don't want to deal with instead of taking the time to just deal with it and move on.

It is so easy for me to write about dealing with the problem. I get it. And I don't know what you are dealing with in your life right now. You've got that right.

I don't know the exact problem that you are avoiding, but I do know that the problem will not just go away. Many times in my life, I've hid behind a display at a store and waited for the person I was avoiding to leave. I am asking you to step out from behind the display and deal with the problem. Dealing with the problem may not make you and the person become friends again, but you do not need to live in fear. And while they may not accept your apology, you need to forgive yourself! Give this problem to God. Give him all the reasons you have been avoiding the issue. Give him all of your excuses and worries. He is big enough to help you sort them out and move toward a healthier way of dealing. I would also add, do not hesitate to find a professional to talk to about the problem. Continue to give God a chance to work and set you free.

The day Jesus met the Samaritan woman, she was going about life as normal. Jill went to the well to get some water a little later in the day in order to avoid the other women. She wanted peace. She was not there for a gossip session. She wanted to get water and get home quickly. When Jesus spoke to her, I am sure her stranger danger radar was in full affect. She would have had huge trust issues.

She used every excuse she could muster, but Jesus waved her excuses away like flies. Her surprise when Jesus talked to her is evidence of her shame. Jesus knew this woman needed a true encounter with God. When you look at how ashamed she was of her life, you see the pain she lived with daily. She was a broken woman. I love that Jesus has no issue with any of her excuses. He even tells her about the things she is most ashamed. He sets her free by speaking the most shameful things in her life aloud. He does not avoid the problems. Jesus gives hope.

The course of Jill's life was forever changed from shame to hope by the Man who spoke truth over her life. No matter what you have going on in your life, Jesus wants to give you hope.

Jesus made this trip to Samaria, to the well, just for her. I cannot prove that theory, although I am sure Jill would agree. Jesus took time to meet her *where she was* that day. We often think we can only meet with God in church or on our knees. Jesus could have gone to the well in the early morning, avoiding the afternoon heat, and if Jill missed the divine meeting, well, that would have been too bad. But Jesus knew. I love that Jesus not only shows us his wisdom in this story, but also his great compassion to meet us wherever we are in life.

God comes to our door and knocks, we only need to open it to him. He knows what and who we're avoiding and why, and will meet us behind the display at the store. The question is, will we set aside our excuses of why we're not worthy of the conversation to hear what he has to say?

God loves to find the lost sheep, and often we are out wandering in pain, unsure of how to get back. Will you stop where you are and listen for the voice of God? He will guide you to a place of safety and love. His love. It may be picking up the Bible and reading the book of John. The voice may be a sermon or a podcast. The key is to listen. God wants to be your source of everlasting water. We are not expected to be in the perfect place to find him, but we are expected to change when we hear his words.

Reflection Verse

Come to me, all you who are weary and burdened, and I will give you rest. Take my yoke upon you and learn from me, for I am gentle and humble in heart, and you will find rest for your souls.

Matthew 11:28-29

three

Precious Princess

Genesis 17:15-18:15

Many of us know Sarah's story of giving birth to Isaac at an old age. But before we dive in, I want to touch on her uniqueness. Sarah was the first woman after Eve to be mentioned in the Bible by name. She is one of the only women for whom we get an accurate age; most others merely get an approximation. Sarah is one of the few women whose name God changes. And while He does change the name of several men in the Bible, women hardly get their names mentioned, let alone changed. I think these few facts show us how special she was to God. She was more than a wife to Abraham and the mother of the nations. She was a child of God. I love that God gave her a name that means princess.

Sarah was married to one of the most famous men in the Bible. I mean, every kid learns the "Father Abraham had many sons" song. Abraham and Sarah have a unique story of being content in very hard situations. If you take the time to read it, you will see their heart. Starting in Genesis 12, two hundred years after the flood, we are introduced to a man and his wife who hear from God. God tells them to leave their settled land and their family to follow after His new plan for them. They take their nephew, Lot, with them on this adventure. God promises Abraham and Sarah that they will be the start of a great nation.

Sarah is a beautiful woman. She is also a woman from whom we hear very little complaints, which makes her even more beautiful and admirable. "Better to live in a desert than with a quarrelsome and ill tempered wife" (Proverbs 21:19). Sarah spends the rest of her life wandering, with no record of driving Abraham crazy by fighting him at every move. I could not find record of her yelling at him about almost sacrificing her son. If someone thought about bringing my only son as a sacrifice, we would be reading about my anger in the Bible. It would *not* have been subtle.

I spent most of my life trying to fade into the background, only making funny comments when I saw an opening. But as time marched on, I started to embrace my outspoken self. A year ago, I was living life, being my outspoken self, when someone told me they had thought I was rude when they first met me. I had made a sarcastic comment in a meeting that was misunderstood by this person. I was really humbled. Sarcasm is my family's love language, but I do not want to be known for being rude, sarcastic or even loud. I took my heart before the Lord and he reminded me of a verse I have hanging in my kitchen. "Even a **fool** who keeps silent is considered **wise**; when he closes his lips, he is deemed intelligent" (Proverbs 17:28).

Let me be clear, I am still working on not acting like a loud mouth, especially when it could get a laugh. I think being funny and outspoken are important, but I am learning the time and place for such things. I need to watch my words; they can cut deep wounds if not carefully used. Being loud and funny is fun, but looking like a fool is not. To help with this, I have started to guard my heart from things that make me think negatively. I have changed what I read, what I watch, and who I hang out with. I've been learning to be kind and thoughtful when I speak. In my experience, surrounding yourself with positive talk makes a big difference in your outlook.

Sarah kept quiet. But Sarah also laughed! I grew up hearing about this old woman who God promised would be a mom, and what did she do when she heard it was actually going to happen? She laughed! We often equate this action with a lack of faith, that she did not believe the word she was given. And while that really could have been the case, I think her action goes deeper.

If someone said to me that God is going to keep his promise to me and will rain down classic jellybeans from the sky, I would laugh. I would laugh thinking "that is ridiculous," and also laugh knowing that God's plan is always so different than what I think it will be. While getting my buckets ready to catch the jellybeans, I would be laughing to myself at God's creativity. I think Sarah's laugh was both. She would have seen God move many times before. She even tried to make his promise come to pass by giving her maidservant to Abraham. Her laugh could have been an "I should have waited for you to show me your plan, Lord" laugh, while shaking her head in awareness of her own disbelief and impatience.

As we all know, Sarah did give birth to a son. She and Abraham named him Isaac, which means laughter. He was a daily reminder that laughter was the answer; Isaac was the answer to God's plan for them. But she did not spend her years of being barren without laughter. She enjoyed her time with Abraham. The only time we see her upset is when she realized she had made her own plan with her maidservant in an attempt to achieve God's promise for her, and that only got ugly.

And while I am not sure that I can say that life was *full* of laughter for Sarah, I think a light and contented heart would have laughed when it heard the Lord's plan. She was a woman God cherished, his precious princess. She was as big a part of Abraham's success as was his own faith. She stood beside him through all of their family feuds, moving from area to area, and raising Isaac. Abraham trusted Sarah, and though she may have made mistakes, her words were powerful.

So often in our world we do not count our words as powerful. We dismiss the idea they impact others, or even ourselves. The Bible tells us that our words have power (Proverbs 15:4). Social media is sometimes seen as an avenue to share our words without consequence, but that's simply not true.

We will be held accountable for every word we type or share, just as I learned the hard way my sarcastic comments were not painting a true picture of my heart. We must be wise with our words, giving great care to what we say to our spouse, children, coworkers, friends—even to strangers at the grocery store! We are called to be the salt and light of Jesus. Jesus spoke his words carefully, and so must we.

Reflection Verses

Whoever guards his mouth preserves his life;
 he who opens wide his lips comes to ruin.

         Proverbs 13:3 ESV

Do not let any unwholesome talk come out of your mouths,
but only what is helpful for building others up according to
their needs, that it may benefit those who listen.

         Ephesians 4:29

Without wood a fire goes out;
 without a gossip a quarrel dies down.

         Proverbs 26:20

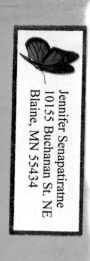

four

Gracious Giver

1 Samuel 1-3

We meet Hannah in I Samuel as her family travels to give sacrifices to the Lord. She is introduced as one of Elkanah's two wives. Her sister-wife, Peninnah, is given a portion of meat for her and ALL of her sons and daughters. And while I could not find an exact amount given to Hannah, who was barren, it's needless to say Peninnah's portion was certainly larger than what was given to Hannah.

As you read the beginning of her story, you see people say hurtful things to her. And even with the best of intentions, words cut deep to the heart. Her husband says, "Am I not worth 10 sons?" Eli calls her a drunk; her sister-wife pokes at the fact she is barren. Hannah continues to seek after God.

So often in life, when words are spoken into our lives, we hold them as truth and let them drive a wedge between ourselves and God, or ourselves and others. When I was twelve years old, my home was stressful. I wasn't doing well at school, mostly because things were falling apart at home. I didn't know it at the time, but my parents were dealing with legal issues. All I knew was that something was wrong, and so I tried to fix it with food. In fact, that year I received my all-time favorite childhood gift: my very own block of Velveeta! Yes, I love food to this day. And though I was never skinny before, I put on a bunch of weight and almost hit 200 pounds that year. My world was crumpling around me and the only thing I had power over was the food I consumed.

During this time, while playing post office in my basement, a friend said to me, "If I was as fat as you are I would kill myself." I laughed it off. Humor was (and is) my favorite weapon, but those words changed the way I lived my life from that day forth. I started down a path of hatred of self and love of food, which is not a good cycle to have as a growing teen (or adult for that matter). I praised myself when I lost weight. I hated myself every time I ate too much. It was a hate/love rollercoaster between food and myself.

Having your self-esteem wrapped up in how many calories you consume or pounds you weigh can take you off the path of hearing from God. The Father loves you no matter your weight. Many live in that place, but God wants to set you free.

It's time to take out that paper or journal. Write down the words that run your life. They can be negative or positive. Scripture, words of a friend, words from a parent. Set aside the time to dig deep and discover the words that are scratched into your heart.

Hannah's heart was heavy. *Barren* was the word etched on her heart. I love that even though she and her scarred heart were not perfect, God saw her in her pain and gave her a son.

The next part of her story is what really baffles me. Hannah, after years of waiting for God to give her a son, gives her son back to God. And not through a dedication service at church—she gives him over to Eli. As in, she sends her only son to live with a surrogate father in the presence of the Lord.

Yes, I know she made a promise to do so when she asked the Lord for a child. But at the risk of sounding sinful, I know I would have tried to wiggle my way out of that promise…

I am sure I must have promised summers only.

I am sure they do not want another mouth to feed.

I am sure God only meant for me to give Samuel to him in my heart, not to physically hand him over.

My mind goes a hundred miles a minute thinking of bad things that could happen without my motherly influence in my child's life. If I had heard even one story of that boy hearing voices in the middle of the night and Eli not snuggling him back to sleep, I would have packed up my momma bear claws and paid them a little visit. Another difficultly of this situation is trusting Eli to be his father figure. Not many of us would consider giving our kids to others to be raised, much less to a man whose own sons were not following God. The thought might be a bit beyond our comprehension.

Hannah is not recorded in the Bible as being a helicopter mom. She didn't hover over everything and everyone influencing her son. Hannah knew Samuel was watched over by God. Eli might have "raised" him, but God was influencing him. God spoke to Samuel at a young age, and so he followed God's voice, not the voice of men.

As we look at our lives and the lives of our children, we must know that people are going to say things that hurt or scar our hearts. Just as I allowed others' words to be etched on my heart, you also may have let others' words be etched on yours. Are you willing to take the words on your heart and give them to God?

God is the perfect Father, and his words have been a balm to heal those words scarred on my heart. God's promises in the Bible have breathed life where there was pain. Do I still struggle with the words I believed for so many years? The honest answer? Less and less, as I cling to God.

God wants to talk to us and raise us. He wants to be someone we trust. But trust is hard. "Trust in the Lord with all your heart and lean not on your own understanding" (Proverbs 3:5) is a piece of scripture I memorized years ago, but I still live my life like I think my way is better. It's one thing to say you trust, and another to live out that trust. It's usually not until I stand humbled from failure or pain that I say, "I trust your way God." God's way may seem to be harder at first glance. But really, when you realize that God loves you and you trust in that love, you will see his way isn't harder, it is the perfect path. You have to trust in God's love for you and believe that He wants the best for you. His way is paved in his wisdom, perfect timing, and love.

Hannah's story teaches us that trust in God is the only way to a life of renewal. She was in tremendous pain and despair, and the Lord was faithful to renew her situation. Because she trusted the Lord, she was able to have many more children and be the mom of the man who spoke for God to an entire country, including anointing its kings.

As we give our scarred hearts to God, I believe he will help replace the negative words in our hearts with His words, just as he did for Hannah. Words like loved, cherished, purposed, and my child in whom I am pleased.

Reflection Verse

More than that, we rejoice in our sufferings, knowing that suffering produces endurance, and endurance produces character, and character produces hope, and hope does not put us to shame, because God's love has been poured into our hearts through the Holy Spirit who has been given to us.

Romans 5:3-5 ESV

five

Fearless Beauty

Esther 1-4

There are several queens mentioned in the Bible, but only one has her own book: Esther. Her fairytale story is full of intrigue, plot twists, and betrayal. Little girls know her name and look up to her still today. She's kind of a big deal.

We join King Xerxes I's party about 400 years after Nineveh is destroyed and 400 years before Julius Caesar, around the time (give or take 50 years) of Ezra and Nehemiah. King Xerxes is feasting and showing off to his friends. He spares no expense; the Bible takes time to describe the opulence in great detail. This party is over the top. The king calls for Queen Vashti and she refuses to come.

Let me note here that we do not know exactly why she didn't go. I like to think it was because she'd seen all this crazy before at his previous parties and she refused to indulge him once again, but because there would have been great consequences for disobeying the king, I imagine she had very good reasons for not joining the party.

Upon receiving the news she would not be joining him, the King is angry and embarrassed. HIS queen did not obey him. He looks foolish to his friends and advisers. She is his property and she has no rights; in fact the advice he gets to respond to her disobedience leads to all women in his kingdom losing their rights. He decrees in every language that every man from the least to the greatest shall be ruler over his own household (Esther 1:20-22).

This is a king with anger issues. It is one thing to take away your queen's privileges, but Xerxes took her title. This event affected all who were under his rule. That must have been some party!

As I read this chapter again, I am so glad that I am not Queen Vashti. She was between a rock and a hard place. Her life was forever altered by this one decision, as were the lives of all the women in Xerxes's kingdom.

Life is not made up of black and white choices. It is hard to navigate through following your gut, finding your voice, listening to God's word, and balancing that against the constant challenges we face in this world. We need to constantly go back to our core belief: God is for us. I am sure Queen Vashti was not following the Bible, but her core values must have been what kept her away from that party.

What are your core values? Take a moment to jot them down.

What do you really believe? Don't write down what you think others would want you to say; take time and dig deep to find what you really believe.

Back to Esther. The movie plot fades to show men roaming the land, looking for beautiful young virgins to join the king's harem. After twelve months of beauty treatments, they have a chance to impress the king. I always think of *The King and I* when I think of this time: lots of women fighting over who will be fancied and others hoping not to be seen. I would have been one of the latter, not wanting to be the next queen of a mad man known for irrational ruling.

Esther is chosen to join the harem and wins favor from the beginning. When the time comes for Esther's turn to visit the king, she takes advice from the king's eunuch in charge of the harem and only brings what he says. King Xerxes thinks she is amazing, just like everyone else who has met her so far. Esther finds favor and King Xerxes makes her his queen.

Sweet Queen Esther has a secret, like any good story plot needs. She is a Jew. Esther was not living in her own land, she was living in exile. She was an orphan without any rights. Her uncle, Mordecai, a rabble rouser. He was not popular in the castle since he would not bow to those who expected him to do so. Esther was smart to keep her secret, as being a Jew and a relative of Mordecai's would not have helped her win any favor.

Her uncle, Mordecai is rude to a man named Haman. Haman takes offense with not only Mordecai, but all of the Jewish people. Using his influence, Haman convinces King Xerxes to kill the Jews in their land.

Now that she's queen, I am sure Esther is minding her own business and trying to stay out of trouble when she hears from her maids and eunuchs that Mordecai is at the gate acting all crazy. Okay, the Bible does not say crazy, but to those who didn't know Jewish customs, it most likely looked crazy. Instead of ignoring the "problem" because of her busyness—she is the queen after all—

Queen Esther sends clothes. This is my kind of woman. I believe a life can be changed by a good pair of shoes! But Mordecai refuses her fashion advice, which would have allowed him entry into the king's gates. Esther could have thrown her hands in the air at his refusal to accept her help, but instead, she takes a small step forward and sends someone to find out what is really going on and hopefully get a grasp on the situation. Mordecai asks her to risk her life to save her people.

Here it is, the pivotal moment in the story. Will Esther step up to the challenge? Or will she step away and hope God has a different plan?

I am a woman who likes adventure and trying new things. I have FOMO! Fear of missing out is a real thing in our culture. We are often afraid of missing out on what others are doing, being left out of coffee with friends, missing a party, or even disappointing a family member. I struggle with always wanting to be there when someone "needs" me, and often place the need to take care of myself on the back burner for so long that I end up burning out. And while it's hard for me to ignore others' asks of me, I can more easily ignore God's. I rationalize that God's plan can wait until I have time. God could have sent his back up in to save the Jewish people, but he gave the opportunity to Esther. She did not make excuses; she stepped into God's plan. I want to be more like that in my life—to understand God's ask of me and start making a plan to make it work.

Esther now has a plan, which, in my humble opinion, is not a great one. My plan might have been a little less "life on the line" and more "let me write a letter." Good thing God chose Esther.

Esther is led by God's grace and the plan works! She saves her people and continues to be in the favor of King Xerxes. Her act of bravery even led to a holiday (Purim) in Jewish tradition. All because a young girl listened to her uncle and was brave, clever, and respectful. You can read her full story in the book of Esther. It's a fun read.

Earlier in this chapter I asked you to take a moment to write down your values. I feel your values (or priorities) charter your life. If you believed the world was flat you would never go on a cruise or travel. Your belief would keep you home, fearing the edge of the world could be somewhere around Colorado.

First, you must deal with the beliefs that are holding you back from being the best you. Are they based in truth or experience? Do they line up with God's word? Do they support the fact that God is for you?

Second, if you believe God is for you, does that make a difference in your life?

Your core values can boost you up to new and greater things or they can hold you back. My prayer is that you'll take time to think about which beliefs are holding you back. I am not huge on self-reflection, because I am not always happy with the truth I find staring back at me. When you're in a dark room, and someone turns on the light without you knowing that it was going to happen, it's startling. Adjusting to the light is not always fun through squinted eyes. Take a real look at your values. Adjusting them to the light will not be an overnight process. You will not wake up the next morning believing the world is round, it is going to take time to believe your new value. You may need to go to the edge of Colorado to see for yourself that it's not the end of the world.

You may need to write down God's promises about you and place them around the house until you really believe that God has a plan for you that includes hope. Be patient with yourself. But most importantly, be honest with yourself and with God. He can handle your core. And when you're ready to believe, He can share His plan for you, if only you take time to listen with an open heart.

Reflection Verse

"Though the mountains be shaken and the hills be removed, yet my unfailing love for you will not be shaken nor my covenant of peace be removed," says the Lord, who has compassion on you.

Isaiah 54:10

six

One in a Thousand

1 Kings 11

Solomon was the third king of Israel. His father, David, was mentioned in the Bible as a man after God's own heart. David did great things and made some big mistakes. Solomon had big shoes to fill, following in his father's footsteps *and* being the king God chose to build the temple, God's first permanent home!

When David was chosen to take the kingdom from Saul, he was an unlikely choice. He was young, without reputation or lineage to the king. After many struggles, it was time to pass the nation of Israel to his son. But Solomon was not the heir apparent; he had older brothers and his mom (Bathsheba) got him into power.

Solomon is known for several things: building the temple, being wise, and having many wives. His father, King David, had eight wives—enough to drive a sane man crazy. Solomon went a bit further than his father and had SEVEN HUNDRED wives and three hundred concubines. A concubine was a wife that was also a servant. Many of the wives were most likely given to him for peacekeeping or trade endeavors, like a chip to bargain or merchandise to trade.

It's hard to even wrap your mind around the number of women in this man's life. I am not sure I know that many people. I've always found it funny that Solomon is known for being wise, as having that many women in your life does not seem wise to me. That many women competing for one man's attention? Sounds like The Bachelor on steroids: drama, "cat" fights, constant chaos.

I imagine that being one of many would be hard. Every woman would need to find her place. Their individual talents and passions were likely lost on King Solomon. He may never have heard them sing, see them paint, or watch their impressive underwater basketweaving skills. The things that made them special, that brought each of them joy, King Solomon likely never knew. All of those deep, intimate feelings, lost in the crowd.

Being a cog in life is not easy. Yes, you make a difference, but you don't always see the whole picture. You likely feel overlooked and undervalued. Some days we all feel this way. Like we're just part of a machine that we don't care much about in the grand scheme of things. I know many that feel this way in church, like you're only filling the pew. Or even worse, working in a ministry or a job just to fill a hole, hating what you do, wanting more. I have good news for you: *there is more*. We are made to be a special part of the church, not just a cog.

My mom used to do lead the donut ministry at my church. Every Saturday night, we went to the church to fill the huge coffee pots and set their timers. Then the next morning, early before Sunday school, she would troop us three kids to the grocery store to pick up donuts and cookies. I loved it because I got to pick out my favorite cookies. Isn't it every kid's dream to walk through the grocery store with six dozen of her favorite cookies and boxes upon boxes filled with every kind of donut you can imagine? It was mine, and it was awesome.

I think my mom liked doing the donut ministry simply because it needed to be done—it wasn't necessarily her passion, but it was a manageable way that she could fill a ministry need. After years of serving donuts, my mom passed it over to one of her friends. Her friend served donuts and coffee every Sunday with a new excitement. The donut ministry was her passion! She took it to a new level, recruited new people to minister to so many in the church, and did such a wonderful job.

My mom was a donut ministry cog, going through the motions every Sunday. After time she needed to find someone else to bring it to a new level because it was their passion.

The women that married Solomon needed to see beyond their marriage for purpose. Even though, back then, a woman's full purpose *was* to get married and produce heirs. Which had to be a little hard to do when they were fighting 999 other women for a little of the king's attention! Some of those wives may have accepted their role as a cog. Others may have found ways to use their talents to make a difference. They had a choice to fight for attention, to sit back and wait for attention, or to find another way to feel fulfilled.

Are you one of 999? Do you feel overlooked and under-appreciated? You could be a mom of toddlers, comparing yourself to other super moms. Find your super power—we all have one! You could be an employee who keeps getting overlooked by more outspoken coworkers. Find your super power. You could be a young person, held back because of your youth. What super power has God given you?

It's time to tap into the special talents, thoughts, and tools that God has given to you, and to you alone! In fact, take some time to write them down right now.

Don't be one of those wives who sits around, waiting for her scheduled time with the king. Make your own story. You do not have to be the top wife to make a difference. You do not need to fight and claw your way to the top—God has a path for you that may not look like others' plans. Take time to hear from God on your next step, so not to become a cog in someone else's plan. It's time for you to step into God's plan for your unique story.

Reflection Verses

And we know that in all things God works for the good of those who love him, who have been called according to his purpose.

Romans 8:28

"Therefore I tell you, do not worry about your life, what you will eat or drink; or about your body, what you will wear. Is not life more than food, and the body more than clothes? Look at the birds of the air; they do not sow or reap or store away in barns, and yet your heavenly Father feeds them. Are you not much more valuable than they? Can any one of you by worrying add a single hour to your life?

"And why do you worry about clothes? See how the flowers of the field grow. They do not labor or spin. Yet I tell you that not even Solomon in all his splendor was dressed like one of these. If that is how God clothes the grass of the field, which is here today and tomorrow is thrown into the fire, will he not much more clothe you—you of little faith?

So do not worry, saying, 'What shall we eat?' or 'What shall we drink?' or 'What shall we wear?' For the pagans run after all these things, and your heavenly Father knows that you need them. But seek first his kingdom and his righteousness, and all these things will be given to you as well. Therefore do not worry about tomorrow, for tomorrow will worry about itself. Each day has enough trouble of its own."

Matthew 6:25-34

seven

Last Chance

Genesis 38

Tamar found in the book of Genesis is not to be confused with David's daughter, Tamar. Both of these women have stories in the Bible that make us uncomfortable and challenge our belief in humanity. For this chapter, we're going to look at Genesis Tamar, who comes on the scene as a woman marrying a man that did evil things. We have no clue exactly what he did, we just know that God was not pleased with him and killed him.

Tamar is now a widow. Not only did Tamar lose her husband, she lost everything: her land, money, and social standing. In those times, a wife was not a benefactor of her husband's inheritance. Everything went to the closest male heir. A son would inherit his father's land if the woman was lucky enough to have one. But in Tamar's case, she did not have children, so her only hope was her husband's brothers.

The law of the time said that her husband's brother could marry her, and if they produced an heir, then that son would inherit the first husband's wealth. The son would count as the first husband's son, not his brother's. With this in place, Tamar married her brother-in-law. He did not like the idea of producing a son who would not legally be his. I think Tamar may not have been thrilled about him, either. The Bible does not say anything to indicate this, but who wants to be passed around just to produce an heir for a man who God saw evil enough to kill? Not a big line for that ride.

Much to her shame, the brother-in-law sins and God kills him, too. Now Tamar has one more brother-in-law with whom to have a son for her first husband. A *young* brother-in-law. As if this biblical soap opera is not weird enough, her father-in-law tells her to wait for her remaining brother-in-law to grow up before she marries him.

I have often thought that Tamar herself was most likely very young as well, maybe even the same age as the "young" brother-in-law. And now she has to wait an undisclosed number of *years* before her life *might* return to *somewhat* normal. She is in a holding pattern.

Waiting is not something I enjoy. Unless it's at a restaurant. When there's a wait at a restaurant I feel like I made a good choice to eat there since everyone else wants to eat there, too. To be honest though, I do not like waiting for my food once I'm seated. You see, I am not super patient.

When I was a child, my family set up our Christmas tree in the basement. I was the only one whose room was in the basement. Yes, you may already see the unwrapping of the story. One year, I decided that waiting was just not for me. I unwrapped most of the presents under the tree that had my name on them, just enough to know what I was getting, and then taped them back together. I remember the thrill of the crime like it was yesterday.

When Christmas morning came, my crime had not been discovered but the excitement of Christmas surprises was lost on me. Yes, I loved my gifts, but my impatience had robbed me of the true joy I had felt on Christmas mornings before. I had to fake my surprise that year.

Tamar was still waiting, not for Christmas, but for her life back. She was living in poverty. Her fate was not in her own hands.

She gets word that her father-in-law is headed her way. Some women might have confronted him. Some may have cried and pleaded. Not Tamar. She finds his weakness and uses it in her favor. The soap opera gets steamier. She disguises herself as a woman of the night and sleeps with him. Not in a restful way, but in a baby-making way. No more waiting around for her.

Tamar became pregnant. She must have been waiting for the word to spread to her father-in-law, knowing he would find out. Gossip is real, people; gossip never stays in one spot, it travels. In her case, she knew it would and that was exactly what she needed.

When her father-in-law heard she was pregnant, he was angry! She had sinned and shamed his sons. She, too, is now a shame to his family name. He knew she must be killed. Time to show him the proof of her "affair"—his own staff, seal, and cord—the very items he had left with the woman of the night for payment. The reveal must have been epic. I can only imagine his confusion, and then his realization of his part in this plot twist.

Tamar gives birth to twins. These twins must have innately known the odd circumstances of their conception, since they appear to be fighting as they leave the womb. At birth, one boy sticks a hand out, which is encircled with a cord. The other baby, his brother Perez, pulls him back in, so that Perez is the one to come out fully first. How unlucky for the brother (Zerah) with a red cord around his wrist! He was pushed out of the way, and his brother Perez took the first-born title from him. The first-born ruled the household and received all of his father's inheritance. Perez is also in the lineage of Jesus.

This very unlikely soap opera in the Old Testament shows us that it is okay to stand up for yourself. You are worth more than being cast aside because you do not fit into someone else's plan. You also need to remember that God is bigger than their plan. God is for you, and you can't let others determine your future. Let God make the path for you.

Reflection Verses

So do not fear, for I am with you;
    do not be dismayed, for I am your God.
I will strengthen you and help you;
    I will uphold you with my righteous right hand.

Isaiah 41:10

Lord, how many are my foes!
    How many rise up against me!
Many are saying of me,
    "God will not deliver him."
But you, Lord, are a shield around me,
    my glory, the One who lifts my head high.
I call out to the Lord,
    and he answers me from his holy mountain.
I lie down and sleep;
    I wake again, because the Lords sustains me.
I will not fear though tens of thousands,
    assail me on every side.

Arise, Lord!
    Deliver me, my God!
Strike all my enemies on the jaw;
    break the teeth of the wicked.
From the Lord comes deliverance.
    May your blessing be on your people.

Psalm 3

eight

Outspoken Sister

Exodus 2, Numbers 12

We meet Miriam as a young girl, during a terrible time in history. She is a slave in Egypt, during the time Pharaoh is having Israel's baby boys killed in order to keep their population down. It doesn't seem like the best time to be alive, but I sense from her a "we got this" attitude. Miriam thinks quick on her feet, has great ideas, and leads at a young age. Clever is the word I have always associated with her.

We do not hear much about Miriam and Moses's mom in this story, which I think is because she's not an obvious star. Moses ends up being a great leader in Israel's history. But I think we should give his mom some credit; after all, she is the one who feeds him physically for the first years of his life and likely prays for him for the rest of it. She did not get to raise him in the way she may have planned. Her dreams for him and his childhood were stolen from her. So while she may not be the big hero in the story, her letting go and sending that baby boy down the river was most likely the hardest thing she ever did. And that act saved the whole nation of Israel.

Now that we've given their mama due credit, let's go back to Miriam. Miriam takes her baby brother down to the river and watches his basket as it floats away. As a kid, I imagined the reed cradle getting caught in whirlpools, being followed by crocodiles, and being landed on by birds curious to see the cargo. Miriam watched it all happen; throwing rocks at the crocs, praying for the flow of the river to stop, and hoping that big bird would find somewhere else to rest. Hours of watching and praying for the basket to settle in the reeds.

A woman yells from the bank for her servants to retrieve the basket. Miriam's heart must have been beating out of her chest; she most likely knew the woman was Egyptian and would have been able to tell by her dress she that she was in the royal court. Worst-case scenario: her baby brother was now in the hands of the enemy, Pharaoh's daughter.

Once again, God had a plan that was bigger than what could be imagined by Moses's family. I am so impressed with Miriam's quick thinking and bravery. She stepped out of her hiding place, taking her and her brother's lives into her own hands. She was a slave after all, and she approaches the princess. Taking a deep breath, Miriam suggests that she knows someone who can help the princess take care of the baby.

When Miriam returned home to tell her mom what had happened, I would guess her mother was full of both excitement and anger. I would have been angry with my daughter for taking such a risk, but simultaneously grateful that she did so.

Fast-forward several years and Moses is now an adult. He loses his temper with a slave master and murders him, then runs away.

Let's step back from the situation and think about it from Miriam's point of view. She risked her life to give her brother a chance to live, and now, after years of being raised in luxury (not slavery like her) Moses commits murder and runs away. *You have got to be kidding me!* I am sure Miriam was angry with Moses for leaving her to deal with the consequences of his actions. Both her people and the slave masters would have likely known there was a connection between the two, even if they did not know their actual relation. Ugh! Being associated with a murderer would have put her on a watch list for both sides. She may have even been labeled a troublemaker.

When I was in high school, I was not the best student…and that might be an understatement. Though I was smart, my interests did not lie with schoolwork! I had a reputation for taking short cuts and not attending classes very often. I may have been the reason some attendance policies were created! Since I attended a small private school, people tended to expect the same from my two younger siblings. Both struggled because of my actions; they had to overcome preconceived thoughts about them. But don't worry; both thrived! The teachers and peers loved them despite my actions. And like Moses, I became a very different person in my adulthood.

Much like Miriam, my siblings had to work harder to prove themselves and establish their own reputations apart from mine (and Moses's). Miriam was her own hero, and sometimes, her own worst enemy. She was a strong woman and a leader in Israel.

Fast-forward a few more years, and just as life's gotten back to a regular rhythm, Moses returns to Egypt with a word from God to disrupt all of their lives. Miriam had a choice to make: she could stand beside her brother or she could stand back and watch to see what would happen next. If you take time to read through the story of Miriam, you will see that she steps up and helps her brother lead the Israelites out of Egypt.

When the plagues were over and the Israelites had crossed the Red Sea, Miriam led the women in worship. Miriam is not a wallflower and she leads people in her own way. Or rather, in the way God created her to. She is spoken about several times in the story of Moses, but never mentioned to be a mother or wife. She is a prophet and a leader of her group. In Israel, Moses led them all, but when you read closer, there are many leaders who served as mouthpieces for the vision God gave Moses.

In Numbers, Miriam and Aaron speak against Moses and his wife, and the Lord invites them into the tent of God. God comes down in a pillar of cloud and is angry that they spoke against His servant Moses. The Bible says God's "anger burned against them" and the cloud lifts, leaving Miriam with leprosy. Man, if this doesn't teach us to be careful about what we say about our leaders or about our younger brother's wife! Aaron (who is not harmed) begs Moses to pray and ask for healing. He does, but the Lord will not heal her until after she fulfills her consequence of being outside the camp for seven days. Then the camp will move.

What is the point of this story? First, Miriam was a leader and her words were listened to by many. She needed to be careful with her words in general, but especially when it came to what she said about Moses. Second, the Bible says both she *and* Aaron spoke against Moses, but she was the only one punished. I am sure there are lots of theological reasons people have come up with over the years for this, but my simple theory is that her punishment was more impactful. Aaron was more of a "yes man" (or Moses's mouthpiece), while Miriam was more outspoken. People watched Miriam to see what she would get away with in many situations.

Miriam is a fun person to watch, from being a young, brave girl by the Nile to leading, alongside her family, a nation into the wilderness. As we think about our lives in comparison to Miriam's, we can see the importance of taking responsibility for our actions. She was a woman who made her own way; she did not let her brother's failures or successes define her life. And with a brother like Moses, that would have been very difficult. She was honored when she died because she was loved for both her failures and her successes.

Miriam didn't let her past define her. What about you? Have you allowed the people around you to dictate the way people perceive you?

As the wife of a pastor, I have struggled with many things. But the biggest is that my husband is a man who lives like he preaches; his closeness to God is sometimes intimidating. I will be frank, I am very different from him. I often fall short of what I would love to be like. I have spent years trying to live in my husband's shadow, hoping no one would ask me to pray. I am not eloquent and I forget the verses I have known all my life when I pray with people.

As I studied Miriam, I was struck that she made a name for herself by listening to her God. God was not just Moses's God, so she followed him too. She knew God, and she chose to follow Him of her own accord. And though she made mistakes (I could fill a book with the mistakes I have made in ministry!), she still continued to lead.

You do not need to be a perfect leader in the church to make a difference. You can lead a small group of friends just as you are today. You can encourage one friend at a time with your flaws. You can lead others, just by being brave enough to follow God the way he made you to follow him!

Reflection Verse

For God is working in you, giving you the desire and the power to do what pleases him.

Philippians 2:13 NLT

nine

Messy Life

Genesis 24-27

By now you know that I am a big believer in God having a plan. He usually doesn't share the whole plan with us, just a step or two at a time. But sending a servant to a foreign land to find the perfect wife for your only son? Now that plan seems a little too loosey-goosey for my taste.

I can understand Abraham not wanting to travel to find a wife for Isaac, he was up in years at this point. But I find it interesting that he sends a servant by himself and doesn't tell Isaac to go with him. The servant does not have many guidelines for what he's looking for in this wife, other than she not be from the area they live in, and that she must be a relative. Not much to go off of when picking a spouse for your master's son. The son on whom he has pinned all of his hopes and dreams, the son in which God promised to flourish like grains of sand. Go find the woman that will make him happy. Make a love match. Big responsibility!

Now I am no expert on matchmaking in the time of Abraham, yet I do love that the servant prayed to God with this wild request, and *before he finished thinking this prayer* Rebecca showed up to the well. If only we all had prayers answered like this one! Before we even finish asking for a new career, our phone rings with a new job and a pay raise. That would be awesome.

Rebecca was no fool; she was a smart woman. She saw the working of the Lord when she heard the servant's request to God and made quick plans to follow him home to Isaac. Her family tried to keep her at home to "get ready." They were probably trying to help her understand how crazy it was to follow this servant home. Rebecca was not afraid and left with the servant.

Isaac was in the field meditating when Rebecca entered his world. She put on a veil. Isaac took her into his mother's tent and married her. This is not a step-by-step plan. This is a whirlwind.

As I read Rebecca's story, I am struck by her ability to just "go with it." That ability makes this first part of her story hard for me to relate to. I am not a spontaneous person, in fact, I do not even like to deviate from the meal plan I have made for the month. Rebecca is a challenge for me, but she is a good reminder that sometimes following God's plan does require spontaneity on our part.

This is where I would normally say "take out some paper and make a list..." Yet, I guess that does not fit the theme here. Instead,, take a moment and listen to God. Be still and hear what he has to say. He may give you an encouraging word or a new adventure. Be willing to do something spontaneous for God.

A fun surprise in this story is that Isaac loves Rebecca and honors her right away. God honored Rebecca's faith and obedience by this simple act from Isaac.

My husband and I have found that God is really good at closing doors in our path. For us, God seems to only open a few doors in our path, likely knowing that my adventurous self would eagerly run to any barely-cracked-open door. At the age of 22, we found it was time to leave the church we had been pastoring. Unsure of our next steps, we started applying to youth pastor positions at other churches. After many rejections, we soon realized this path was not for us. As far as we could see, our path only had closed doors... what were we to do? Yep, we did what any respectable adults would do: we moved in with my mom. It was so deflating. We went from a lead pastor of a church to now living in my mom's basement with no jobs.

Rebecca's story is not without its own challenges. She is barren for 20 years. Twenty years! After 20 years, I think she deserves a great baby shower and fun pregnancy, but she gets neither. Rebecca gets a word from God about her babies being the heads of two nations who will fight for generations to come. *That* is how she found out she was having twins. No sweet ultrasound and magical gender reveal for her.

After waiting for 20 years, I might have been upset by this news. For 20 years, I would have dreamed of a baby who slept through the night at two days old. A son who shadowed his dad, played in the mud and loved to shower afterwards. You know, all those dreams you have before reality hits you with a smelly, not sleeping, do-his-own-thing boy.

Rebecca was in for a ride with her boys. They were as different as night and day, and I am sure fought more than we can even imagine. Though Rebecca would have dreamed of perfection, I am sure she learned to lean on God more with her two sons being in constant turmoil.

God's plans are not always easy. I am confident that if I were perfect, the path God had originally planned for me would have been much easier than the path I take daily. The trials of life are where we learn the most valuable lessons. The lessons my husband and I learned in my mom's basement changed the direction of our lives. We learned the path that God had for us was not like that for "normal" people. God had called us to do things outside of the "normal" church.

Rebecca was tasked to raise two boys who would lead nations. The boys would have both been strong-willed children, neither settling for second place. Each son wanted what the other one had. They even fought over meals. Rebecca must have gone grey at an early age with all that yelling.

The Bible tells us that Rebecca loved Jacob, who was quiet and stayed near the tents, and Isaac loved Esau, who liked to hunt and be outdoors. This might have provided a little sanity in Rebecca's world; one boy staying home while the other goes outside to hunt. Nurturing the second born, whom God had said would be the leader of the two, might have been a fun challenge. On the surface Esau would seem the dominant brother. He was rugged and strong, and while he was loved by his father, he did not listen to him. If he had, he would have known not to marry a Canaanite woman. Remember how his grandpa sent a servant away to find Rebecca? Esau did not listen to the family stories. I guess he was too busy playing in the woods. Jacob, on the other hand, stayed close to the tents and knew the stories. He may have even known the words God had spoken when Rebecca was pregnant.

Rebecca helped Jacob get the blessing he needed to become the nation of Israel. We can argue about her motives and actions being under handed. Without Rebecca's help, Jacob would not have received the blessing to rule over his brother. Rebecca's life was messy.

Our lives are messy too. Sometimes we find ourselves in the basement, without a penny to our name. We live our lives in the best way we know how, following God's voice. As we walk through our life, we need to remember that God's plan is not always wrapped with a red ribbon under the Christmas tree. His plan may be the one wrapped by a child, with ripped and crumpled paper. Adventure with God comes in all shapes and sizes. You must be willing to look beyond the wrapping and find the plan God has for you!

Reflection Verse

"Remember not the former things,
    nor consider the things of old.
Behold, I am doing a new thing;
    now it springs forth, do you not perceive it?
I will make a way in the wilderness
    and rivers in the desert.

Isaiah 43:8-9 ESV

ten

Mother of a King

2 Samuel 11-12

Bathsheba. Just the mention of her name brings uncomfortable thoughts and questions to mind. When I think of her name, I don't think of joy and happiness. I think of sin and disappointment. And since we only have a few stories about her in the Bible from which to draw our conclusions, I'm not sure this is entirely fair to her.

Bathsheba's lineage is very impressive. Her father was a highly respected man in King David's army and her grandfather gave council to King David—both revered for their godliness. Bathsheba even married a man that is shown to be great: one of King David's mighty men, a highly respected soldier named Uriah. She is one of the few women mentioned in the lineage of Christ. Her life was simple and full of comfort. Her family was part of the king's inner circle, their house close to his palace, so we can assume she had wealth.

How did things go so terribly wrong?

Though I've heard a great number of theories about Bathsheba, I'm unable to shake the compassion I feel for her. You may not totally agree with my theory, but I think we can all agree that God has a plan for her, despite the sin surrounding her story.

Bathing on her rooftop may seem scandalous, but scripture notes it was wartime. The men and the king were supposed to be at war. King David should not have been peeping around from his rooftop. Bathsheba was getting clean, which most likely was less of a sensual bath and more of a hygiene bath, to follow the words God had given to his people about a woman's monthly cycle. If she was looking to have an affair with the king, there were easier ways to get his attention.

Whatever the motive behind her rooftop bath at dusk, her life is forever changed when King David summons her to his home. Could she have refused? We don't know this answer for sure, but my guess is no. Saying no to the king is not a popular choice, even today. And David knew her father and husband well, so what if he had news about them to share with her? In any case, she went. And whether willingly or by authoritative force, a baby was made that night.

Judgment is something we all deal with in life. Sometimes it's justified, but more often than not it's passed in ignorance of the real story. A young wife at 21 years old, I had the privilege of traveling to Sri Lanka with my husband and his parents. That trip changed my life forever! I got to meet my husband's grandma, who gave me advice I still cherish today. I experienced a culture that changed my perspective on poverty. My world became bigger than the 30-mile radius around my home, and I left a piece of my heart there in Sri Lanka.

When I returned to Minnesota, I shared some of my experiences with others in the church. I was so excited about what

I had learned. I shared about how I had entered a Buddhist temple, not to worship, but to witness their culture. In sharing that experience, I found that I accidentally offended some in my church, and some even rebuked my action of entering the temple.

I don't regret having entered that temple. I was so changed by that experience, watching the poor, lost people worship a statue of a sleeping god. Buddha was sleeping, and these people hoped he would hear their calls for help between snores.

My God is always there for me. He's never shown me a "do not disturb" sign. My heart was broken for these people, and then again when those in my home church spoke judgment about my "wrong" actions.

Just like Bathsheba, people made assumptions about the situation. We cannot know her heart or her frame of mind. We only see her mourning for her husband and baby. She lost everything that evening. King David had her husband killed, and then God puts their son to death to punish David for his sin. Throughout history, Bathsheba has been labeled as the woman who slept with King David. Before that fateful night, she was in a good place, and with that one act, she lost her husband, her reputation, and her baby.

Bathsheba was forever changed because of her night with King David. They both lost their son and the Bible says it was because of King David's sin. This baby was Bathsheba's first born, and she mourned deeply. What a heartbreaking way to be introduced to motherhood. But this loss is not the end of her story.

If we look closer, we do see God's hand at play here. God gives Bathsheba the honor of being in the lineage of his son, Jesus. Solomon was not the heir apparent to the throne after his father, he was chosen because of his mom. Solomon's brothers who were next in line were set to the side by the influence Bathsheba had over King David and his advisors (read 1 Kings 1).

Bathsheba may have been wronged in this situation, but she did not let it define the rest of her life. She must have worked hard to gain favor with both the king and his advisors. Bathsheba proved that she was bigger than her past. She may have come to the palace in shame, but in the end, she helped shape a king.

We need to remember that our past does not define us. It can be hard to move past reputations and labels, but God may have kings for us to shape. These kings may be our children, they may be others in our lives. God does not want us to live in the shame of sin. He doesn't want anything—especially that—to hold us back from His plans for our lives. Plans to use *your* life to show *His* glory to those around you. If we humbly see our sin, our mistakes, our failures, and our disappointments as places to learn, we can grow beyond these circumstances.

How are you going to handle the judgment of others?

Are you ready to step beyond your past to make a difference?

Can you step into the new path God has for you?

Reflection Verse

Remember not the former things,
nor consider the things of old.
Behold, I am doing a new thing;
now it springs forth, do you not perceive it?
I will make a way in the wilderness
and rivers in the desert.

Isaiah 43:18-19 RSV

eleven

Companion

Genesis 25:1-7

In Genesis, there's a short little paragraph tucked in between Sarah's death and before the story of Isaac's wife and family. This paragraph tells us that Abraham, who was 137 years old when Sarah dies, marries again after her passing. Why in the world would a man of that age be looking for a new wife? And not just any wife, but a wife young enough to give him more children. Oh my, when I read this, my idea of gracefully accepting old age was blown. There was no peaceful retirement for Abraham. After more than 57 years of marriage to Sarah, he marries Keturah, and lives for another 38 years.

Because she gave him six more sons, it's likely that Keturah was significantly younger than Abraham. No woman close to his age, without God's intervention, would have been able to conceive and give birth to six boys.

We don't learn much about Keturah in this paragraph, but we read that she was a concubine. A concubine was a servant taken as a wife. In my humble opinion, she was needed to help care for Abraham in his old age. Keturah must have been more than a servant to Abraham; she likely became his companion.

So let's think of Keturah as a caretaker. Someone who was more than a servant to the family. To marry Abraham after he lost the love of his life, she must have been someone he trusted a great deal. Maybe he wasn't looking for a love match, mut more likely for friendship. We of course do not know why he had more sons at the age of 137, but I love the fact that even after a full life with Sarah, his story was not over.

So often in life, we reach an age or milestone and feel we are done. Not done with living, just done with goals and trying new things. My grandmother was not one of those people. She shrunk with osteoporosis and could no longer see over the steering wheel, yet the day she died I found her driver's license on her because she never knew when she might have needed to go for a joy ride. She was always trying new things as she got older, though she was no longer aware that her "new" things were indeed old. But boy, did she teach me to keep trying and setting goals. No matter how many limitations the doctors or her body gave her, she found a way to make sure she was always moving. Always doing something. She did crossword puzzles until the day she died. Nothing was going to stop her from living life to the fullest.

Keturah was Abraham's ticket to this lifestyle in his old age. Their marriage allowed Abraham to have young kids around again, which can make you feel old and tired *and* young and tired at the same time. Can I get an amen?! Keturah was a fresh start for Abraham. She was most likely aware that her role was not to replace Sarah, but to make a new life for her and Abraham together. I imagine with six sons, laughter and energy would have been brought back into their home.

Keturah is someone we know very little about, and though her sons did not inherit Abraham's wealth, he did provide for them and Keturah. What joy she must have brought to an old widower in the last years of his life. What a hard job.

I think she must have been a big blessing to both Abraham and to Isaac.

The death of a dream can be much like losing a person you love. For some of us, we never get over disappointments or failures. We do not move forward, clinging to the good old days. The victories of the past are where we go for comfort, unwilling to try for new victories after a defeat. Abraham had some highs and lows in his life with Sarah. Looking back at what God had brought them through, together, could have been enough for him. But Abraham steps into the future. He puts himself out there, takes a risk and marries Keturah. After the blessing of six more sons, Abraham dies at 175.

Why do we not move into the new things in front of us? What holds us back? Why do we hesitate to step out of our pain or into something uncomfortable? The old dream was a known part of our life, and even though its death may be painful now, consistency and familiarity are appealing when what lies ahead is unknown.

Are you staying in the past as a strategy to not get hurt again? Are you convinced this new idea will fail, just because the last few have? Are you going to live in the past, forever?

I encourage you to pray about this new idea, plan or even person in your path. Does God have a new journey for you that might be scary and full of the unknown? If you will take that small step forward, God will be faithful to hold you in His hands. He is, after all, our Father who wants us to have a full life. I know I want my daughter to live life to the fullest. I don't want her to stay in high school forever because it was amazing, or skip college because she had a bad experience in high school. Just because you have one bad date does not mean you stop dating and decide to be single.

I know you are reading this, thinking that I don't know how bad it was, and you are right! I don't know your story, but I do know that God did not make you to live in your pain or to give up on your dream because of a bad experience. He has bigger plans for you, and he will use your story.

Reflection Verses

Commit your work to the Lord,
and your plans will be established.

Proverbs 16:3 NIV ?

He says: "For I know the plans I have for you, declares the Lord, plans to prosper you and not to harm you, plans to give you hope and a future."

Jeremiah 29:11

twelve

Judge with a Tree

Judges 4-5

Many judges in the Bible have a few paragraphs written about them in the book of Judges. Deborah has two whole chapters. She was a woman of great influence. The Israelites lined up around the block for her counsel. People called her a prophetess, warrior, and poet. She has quite the resume, though details about her personal life are vague.

Deborah is the fourth judge of Israel and the only female judge we know about. The story around her is spectacular. Too good to miss, her story is full of prophecy, leadership, songs, and a big plot twist.

It's fun to imagine Deborah as a five-foot, small-framed, soft-spoken woman, who took instructions from no one but God. Bigger than her body in spirit and might! But from Judges chapters 4-5, I imagine she was a tall, broad-shouldered woman with a dark complexion and dark, piercing eyes. Whatever Deborah looked like, she gained the respect of the people. She was a spokesperson of God.

Picture Deborah, under her palm tree—really, she had a palm tree named the Palm of Deborah in Judges 4:5; crazy cool—giving advice and judgments with birds singing a song for her. You know heroines have birds follow them in song! Sitting under her tree, she heard from God and sent a message to Barak. This message was not just any message, it was big. I am sure I would have asked some follow-up questions of God before sending a message like, "time to get 10,000 soldiers and attack the enemy" to a general. But Deborah is clear in her direction and does not get flustered by the message. She is sure God has spoken.

Deborah must have been practiced in listening to God's voice to be so confident she had heard him clearly. This was not a guess that God might be saying attack. She was clear of what God had spoken to her. Day after day, she surely relied on God's voice to direct her in many decisions. She sat under her palm and listened to God in her everyday dealings. When an argument came to her, she had God's wisdom to share with others.

Do you hear God's voice clearly? A better question might be, do you practice hearing God's voice and direction in the little things in life? When the kids are arguing, do you take a moment to hear God's direction or correction? Yes, this seems impossible, as life comes at you fast and crying children need swift action. As do situations at work. Yet, if we take time to hear God before we get into the quick action moments, God will show us his direction in the crunch times. Take a deep breath in those moments and quiet your heart before the Lord. You may not hear anything, but you will at least have taken the time to refocus on Him.

Many years ago, I was in the car driving and felt the need to take the long way home from work. Home is where the comfy pants are, and I always want to get there quickly. But this day, I ignored the call of the comfy pants, listened, and detoured down a road that would eventually get me home. Then I felt that I needed to pull over. Confused, I pulled my car over and stopped in a random neighborhood. I listened to music and waited for God to move.

My phone rang. I was excited and wondered what adventure God had for me that day. I answered my flip phone to hear my husband on the other end of the line. Yes, it begins! My husband has sold something to a friend and I was a block away from their home. It wasn't necessarily the huge adventure I was hoping for, but it was cool to see how God had placed me in just the right spot.

This small task of listening to God didn't have a huge impact at the time, but it was a building block of faith for me to know that I had heard from God. The next time I heard or felt God ask me to do something, I would know what it was like to listen and obey.

And while I know that, I'm not sure I am ready to relay a message to a 4-star general to gather the troops and attack Canada. But Deborah was ready. Barak's response? "I will only go if you go with me." Oh my, no thank you, I am good with gravy on my fries and Canadian bacon! Wait...that was not her response. Deborah says, "very well, but because you need me to go, the glory will not be yours but a woman's."

Cool, Deborah will get the credit for this victory. I can get on board with this plan.

(I love when we think we know what the plan is, yet God has a different ending in store.)

During the battle, a woman the enemy king trusted took a tent peg and drove it through his head. The scriptures do not give us motive as to why she killed him. We only know he is exhausted, went to sleep, and told, Jael, to not let anyone know he was there. We can only guess her reasoning for killing him herself. Jael forever goes down in history as the woman who defeated the enemy of Israel, and she gets the glory for the victory.

After this strange battle, Deborah wrote a song that details the need for attack and praises Jael. Then, the Bible says Israel has peace for 40 years. All in a good day's work.

Deborah's act of listening to God and leading with Barak leads to 40 years of peace. Something that was unheard of in this ever war-torn area of the world.

It's time we each find our own palm tree under which to sit and listen to God's voice, so that our decisions can lead to 40 years of peace. Though most days, 40 minutes would be a miracle! The good news is that our God is in the business of miracles.

What details are you willing to let God direct?

Find a place where you can rest in God, and learn to hear His voice in the quiet moments. He will have you start with small things, and then, when the time comes and He asks you to go into battle, you will be ready to hear His direction.

Reflection Verse

"The Lord directs the steps of the godly. He delights in every detail of their lives."

Psalms 37:23 NLT

thirteen

Perfectionist

Luke 10:38-41; John 11; 12:1-3

Martha was the hostess with the mostest. The very first Martha Stewart. Written about by both John and Luke, she seemed to have it all together and must have made quite the impression. Even though we always hear her clumped together with her sister, Mary, Martha is always the hostess.

She has two famous stories told about her, but it's clear that her home was one where Jesus and his disciples enjoyed spending time. I like to think of her as an unofficial, female disciple. She may not have sat at the feet of Jesus like her sister, but you can imagine how much she learned with every meal she served Jesus. Martha was an insider; she was one of Jesus' friends, not just a follower.

The closer you get to someone, the more you see them for who they really are, good or bad. In Martha's relationship with Jesus, the more time she spent with him, the more she believed that he was who he said he was. Jesus was always the person he proclaimed to be, whether preaching to a large crowd or with people at a small dinner party. He was a rock who never wavered and always loved.

In life we encounter fake news, fake people, and fake leaders. It makes it hard to believe that you can fully depend on anyone. I learned a lesson about how easily we can be deceived at a young age. I tried a yummy-looking piece of fruit…that ended up being soap! How upsetting it was to not even be able to trust my own eyes.

I'm sure you've all been there, though maybe you weren't foolish enough to think a delicious piece of fruit would be in a bathroom. We have all been fooled before. Our trust waivers when we meet people who end up being very different from what we originally thought. It is hard to find people who are the same at home and in public. I believe this is part of our problem with trusting God: it is hard for us to fathom that someone is who he says he is, all the time. He is the same yesterday, today and tomorrow. The real question is, do you really believe that God can be good and for you all the time, even when you do not believe in yourself?

When our circumstances get bad, we are quick to blame God or ask how he could allow these things to happen to us. God is not a piece of soap impersonating a fruit; He is compassion and love through every season of life. God is still who He is written to be in the Bible. If you are struggling with knowing who He is, read your Bible. You will see person after person in a tough spot find comfort and help in God.

Martha's friendship was suddenly tested. She does not have blind faith in Him, which to me makes her devotion to Jesus all the more significant. She and Mary sent word to Jesus when their brother got sick. They heard nothing. Here Jesus is healing random people all over Israel, and they couldn't get him to come help their brother. I imagine they felt completely forgotten, wondering if He was coming to help. The low point of a friendship is feeling like you are not valuable to someone. Martha would have felt overlooked by her friend. She knew that if Jesus showed up he could heal her brother. So where was he? So help him if he was having a party at another tax collector's house while her brother was dying...

Martha was doing everything she knew to help, but still helplessly watched as her brother slipped away. How many times did she cry, "Where are you Jesus?" It was one thing when her brother was too sick to work, but now he could only lay in bed, barely able to eat. The situation was getting serious.

Martha's brother eventually died, and her sorrow was overwhelming. Watching her healthy brother go from strength to death was more than she could handle. She must have been exhausted from her efforts to keep him alive, and from the extreme grief of his loss, and now she had to prepare for life without her brother. Just getting out of bed must have been a struggle. And now she needed to prepare for his burial, not to mention also taking care of her sister Mary. In Martha's mind, she is the strong one and Mary is just a blubbering mess.

Just when the ordeal was over, in waltzes Jesus. Martha's brother was already dead, and *now* Jesus comes. Martha did not yet know the end of the story. She only knew her pain. And having Jesus show up in the midst of your pain is a miracle. His love for this family was evident, and Jesus was there to help.

We do not always see the whole picture. Often we are stuck in our pain and when Jesus shows up, we are angry he was not there for the struggle. *What good is it to have you here now?*

First, unlike Martha, we have access to Jesus at any time. Second, if someone is going to show up late to your funeral, you want it to be Jesus. Jesus can do miracles. That friend from high school? Well, their tardiness is just annoying.

Jesus did show up to the funeral of his good friend, and he knew he wasn't too late. I am sure Jesus knew Martha's frustration and sorrow, and he came as a friend to comfort. In this situation, he comforted the family by raising Martha's brother from the dead. What miracle might Jesus do in the midst of your pain?

Martha is known for being the woman who worked while her sister sat and chatted with Jesus. She was busy making everything perfect, just as I imagine I would have been. Jesus went to a funeral when he could have performed a simple healing miracle at the house. He was not looking for the perfect situation. I think he scolds Martha for working as a reminder that her friendship was what was important to him, not the perfect meal.

I always know I have a true friend when I go to their home and they open a bag of chips and just put it on the table. No bowl, just a bag of chips. First, because a true friend shares chips! Second, because they feel they can just be themselves—no fancy bowl required—and just chat over delicious chips.

I think Jesus is like this, too. He doesn't need chips in a pretty bowl to visit; I think he likes a messy house. When Jesus showed up to Martha's home after her brother's death, life was as imperfect as it could get. Just as he was there for her in the mess, he is there to help us with our messy lives, too. Our mess and imperfections don't scare him away. Jesus is looking for the kind of relationship that invites him in, serves a bag of chips on the table, and hands him a broom.

It's time to invite Jesus in to help with your mess. Give him permission to help clean. Give him permission to sit down in your mess and chat over a bag of chips. A true relationship can be built when you are at your messiest.

Reflection Verses

The LORD will fight for you; you need only to be still.

Exodus 14:14

"Martha, Martha," the Lord answered, "you are worried and upset about many things, but few things are needed—or indeed only one. Mary has chosen what is better, and it will not be taken away from her."

Luke 10:41-42

fourteen

Survivor By Faith

Joshua 2

This chapter is going to be fun. We are diving into the life of a woman of the night. To put it bluntly, Rahab was a prostitute. She was a well-known woman who hosted men, and she had both influence and money. The Bible mentions her even being approached by the King of Jericho. Her home and business were part of the city wall. People knew her and watched her.

One day, two spies from Israel came to her home. We can only guess how they chose her home; I think it was the only one with a neon "open" sign blinking. This single visit would change the course of her life. She found herself in a situation where she had to trust in a God that she had only heard rumors about, or be loyal to her city. It would be a hard to put my faith in rumors.

She tells the spies she has heard of the great things the God of Israel has done. The stories of the Red Sea and Israel's other victories were part of God's plan to intimidate the people and kings of other cities. Jericho was highly defended and seemingly impossible to defeat. Its high, thick walls were what they had faith in. Rahab thought the walls were no match for this God of Israel.

We do not know how easily Rahab made her choice to help the spies. I imagine it was a hard choice that many would not have the guts to make. I have a hard time just choosing from a menu at a restaurant. I break into a sweat as I try to quickly make the right decision so everyone doesn't wither away from hunger because I took too long to order. I guess I would have crumpled in Rahab's place, while I tried to decide between pizza or a cheeseburger. How thankful the spies must have been that they didn't choose Helen's place down the wall, who would have just curled up into a ball crying! God placed the spies in the home of a woman who was used to making quick and confident decisions. She was prepared for this interruption.

Rahab's boldness in asking for help from the spies is a fun thing to see in a biblical character. So often we see so much hesitation from people who ask for things that we're not sure they even know what they're asking for. Rahab asked for her life and the life of her family members, in exchange for helping the spies. Smart woman! I am not sure she fully understood her ask at the time, as her home would be destroyed and the people of Jericho dead. Her bravery is one reason I believe we read about her several times in the Bible.

Rahab helps the spies escape, not knowing if they can honor their side of the deal. For all she knows, the leaders of Israel could back out of the deal and kill her along with everyone else. What a risk she took.

Risks are a part of life that many of us try to avoid. God has called us to be salt and light to the world, and salt and light can only make a difference when they are applied. We spend most of our lives hoping to blend in, to not be a freak. Even those who seek attention occasionally have places they want to hide. Yet, I think the thrill seekers of life have the right answer. God did not call us to go unnoticed. He called us to adventure with him. When the disciples went out to tell people about their friend Jesus, they didn't hope that only a few select people would notice them. They went out to make a splash. I'm not saying we all need to be preaching on a street corner, but think about the last time you took a risk. I don't mean ordering-lobster-at-a-burger-joint risk. I mean a following-God's-voice risk. Talking to a coworker about an event at church. Stepping into kid's ministry (they *always* need help!).

Rahab's story does not end when the walls of Jericho fall. Her risk paid off. She and her family did as the spies said and were saved. Jericho and all of its people were destroyed. Rahab's whole world was gone, but she was saved because of the faith she had in a God that she did not yet personally know.

You cannot give up when your world is destroyed. God still has plans for you. You may feel useless in your new reality, like Rahab who is called a harlot. But God's love for you goes beyond your current circumstance.

Life after Israel's victory is when things get really hard for Rahab. Her "profession" is most likely known throughout Israel. She knows nothing about Israel's customs or beliefs, their many rules to follow to be clean. Rahab was far from clean in any part of her life. This new way of living was not just a 180-degree turn to make—this was a complete makeover. She had to learn the rules and customs, and then figure out how to get her family to believe as well. And back then, it was not as easy as it is now. We confess and ask for forgiveness through the blood Jesus shed for us. Rahab needed to understand sacrifices, learn a new language, and live in the wilderness.

Rahab went from being a wealthy woman living on the wall and to an outcast. She lived outside of a camp of people who destroyed her city and friends. The hard work and dedication it would have taken from her to become a part of the people of Israel is hard to fathom.

A chapter or two later, Israel loses a battle because of someone's sin. How quickly the people of Israel could have blamed Rahab and her family, the unclean newcomers, for their loss. She was not in a cozy place. She had risked it all for a chance to know the God who loved his people.

I have not done many risky things in my life. In fact, I am a chicken at heart. But the one thing I have is faith. I believe for miracles. I believe God is for me and wants to give me good things. I have prayed for crazy things. For example, when my husband wanted to plant a church I asked God to show me a tree being uprooted. The next week, God uprooted a huge tree, with no storm. I knew God wanted us to plant a church. I drove by that fallen tree for years and it reminded me that God had a plan.

The craziest thing I've ever done in faith was to get my picture taken. Yep, I'm the wild one! Months earlier, I had a dream about being pregnant, in front of the Liberty Bell in Philadelphia. We had been married for nine years with no child to show, and this dream was my hope. We went on a trip with my family to Philadelphia, and I took a pregnancy test the morning we were to visit the Liberty Bell, so sure I would see those two lines. Nope; not pregnant again! But when we got to the Liberty Bell, I asked my husband to take my picture. He was sure this was a bad idea. I was not pregnant, but I had faith in what God had shown me and I knew I needed to take this picture. I shed a tear (or five) and enjoyed the rest of our trip. Months later, I found out that I was indeed weeks pregnant when I was standing in front of the bell.

Rahab ends up not only becoming part of Israel, but she becomes part of the lineage of Jesus. She is mentioned in Hebrews 11, the Faith Chapter, as a hero of faith, despite the label of prostitute. She didn't let her past define her, and you shouldn't either. Take risks. Follow that next step that God has called you to do.

Take that crazy picture!

Reflection Verse

Now faith is confidence in what we hope for and assurance about what we do not see. This is what the ancients were commended for. By faith we under-stand that the universe was formed at God's command, so that what is seen was not made out of what was visible.

Hebrews 11:1-3

fifteen

Swimming with the Fishes

Jonah 2:10

This chapter is written by a different author, from a different perspective: my daughter, Samantha. Hold on to your hats because we are going on a swim with a fan-favorite character from the Bible. Be ready for it to rock your boat.

Hi! This is Samantha and I'm blessed to be Jennie's daughter. When my mom first started writing this book, I was on a mission to come up with as many obscure Bible characters as I could to help her with what I knew would be a great book. But I was stuck. An aspiring evangelist and novelist of pre-teen literature (might as well make your dream career sound fancy!), I pride myself on creativity.

One night lying in bed, with the book of Psalms playing in the background, I had a spark of creativity. I quickly texted my mom my idea, and she suggested I run with it. And so, here we are.

79

Let's take a little break from the harrowing lives of these biblical women and take a more humorous turn. Today's Bible character is enormous; no, not Goliath, but maybe even 15 times his size. She is a good swimmer, basically lives in water.

Any guesses? Did I mention she has fins? Yep, it's a fish. As in Jonah's fish. I would call it an obscure character—we don't even know it's species, much less it's gender, but for our purposes, she is a female whale named Bertha.

Okay, imagine for a moment you're walking (swimming) in the shoes (or fins) of our friend Bertha. You're minding your own business, snacking on krill, when all of a sudden, a male human washes into your mouth. (You might know him as Jonah.) He doesn't taste good at all; completely filled with regret, anger, and fear. Swallowing him was not enjoyable.

Imagine having someone sitting inside you. It would be like having a bad stomach bug or that feeling of something stuck in your teeth. I mean, it isn't fair that you have to suffer because of this man's mistakes.

Some of us can really identify with Bertha in this moment. Not having an obsession of krill, but suffering because of someone else's mistakes. They may drive you crazy, but you're stuck with them. Sometimes, God puts people in our lives so that we can help them in their relationship with Jesus. Sometimes that's supporting them in a crisis, and sometimes it means being the bad guy.

Though I may not have as much experience with this as most, I do go to a public school with a bunch of middle schoolers, who sometimes get on my nerves. Love you classmates, but even my best friends drive me crazy sometimes. And when this book was being written, there was a little thing called COVID-19 going on. When I finally went back to school, I found out that we would now be with the same 10 to 12 people every hour of the day. I tend to have very little patience and be easily annoyed, so I kind of understand Berta's frustration here. Back to the story.

You're an irritable whale and Jonah isn't even happy you saved his life. You try every possible thing to get rid of him (we'll spare the details), but it is almost as if something or someone is protecting him.

It's the second day now and you are tired, just sick of this pest. You even had to give up going to your whale friend's birthday party. If Bertha had been given one wish, I bet she wouldn't have hesitated to be rid of Jonah, or for him to at least stop banging on her ribs. Then, out of nowhere, you feel a sense of peace, patience, and direction. You suddenly feel an urge to turn and swim in the opposite direction. So you do. You head to Nineveh.

I once had similar experience to Bertha, but during a game of floor hockey. I had fractured my wrist three weeks prior, so I couldn't be the floor hockey rock star I normally am. (You don't know me well, so I need to let you know that's pure sarcasm.) I mostly watched the game, barely played, and started to categorize my peers.

Suddenly, like God took off my blinders and gave me his sunglasses, I began to see my classmates the way God sees them. God's love showed me who my classmates were: insecure teenagers, just like me, but without the aid of Jesus. Every human on this earth struggles with insecurities and fear, just like you and me.

God doesn't usually give us direction, peace, joy, patience, or hope without us asking or seeking His Spirit first. We often need to pray first. We have to pray for ourselves, which isn't selfish at all. We have to ask God to help us be a light to the person he's put in our path. We have to ask him to show this person to us in the way he sees them. We have to humble ourselves and ask him to take over.

Trust me, I know this isn't easy. I definitely struggle with this but God knows way better than we do. He loves us so much, and he loves all the people we can't stand.

Which leads to the next really important thing: to pray for that person (Matthew 5:44). Some of you, like me, might not feel you can really influence the person in your path. But do you know what we can all do? Pray. No matter who you are, you can pray. Pray for those who have hurt you. Pray for those who are drifting away from God. Pray for non-believers. Pray for believers to be strengthened through God. Before I go to bed every night, I pray for my friends, spiritual leaders, pastors and the people who annoy me. It's not easy sometimes, but it will deepen your empathy for them.

Back to being Bertha—when you finally get to Nineveh, you hear a voice. A gentle, firm voice orders you to spit out the man. Hooray! You do what all good whales do and spit him out (see Jonah 2:10). You are free. Sweet, sweet freedom. You can be your own fish now! You are so relieved and now you have your appetite back to go feast on krill. Best day ever!

Bertha's story teaches us that even though it can be tough to deal with people, we need to take courage, listen, and trust God to guide us in the direction of his plan. Now, I totally understand how hard it is to learn to listen to God, but the important thing is to be ready and willing to switch course whenever he tells you.

Our journey as Christians is two fold: our journey with God and our journey with people. You can't really excel at either without the other. None of us are trapped in a cave, hanging out with God. People are a part of life and God wants us to love them. You'll come across people you don't like, people you disagree with, and even people who hate you, but Jesus still calls us to love them.

We need to trust that God is for us. We can't judge anyone by their mistakes; we have no idea what insecurities, fears and trials they battle. We have to give them grace like Jesus did. Because God calls us to love Him, and people (Mark 12:31).

It's not always easy. It's not always fair, and it's usually pretty tough. But if you ask Bertha and Jonah, they are both better for their time together. And if you feel like you keep pouring into people without getting anything in return, find encouragement in Galatians 6:9: "So let's not get tired of doing what is good. **At just the right time we will reap the harvest of blessing if we don't give up**" (NLT).

I love this verse. Reread the last part one more time. I constantly need this reminder when things get tough and I am tired of doing the "right" thing. But we have to trust that God will provide and use our imperfections for His glory. **We don't need to be perfect to be loved by God**.

Some of you reading this will find yourselves at Nineveh. Maybe these people are not healthy for you and you need to spit them out. Maybe they have arrived at the destination God is calling them to, and you need to push them out of the nest. You can't hold people from God's divine purpose, and that might require you to cut the rope. Maybe it's time to take a break from a person and put yourself first; remember you've got to love your neighbor as yourself (Matthew 22:39).

If you aren't sure of your next steps, ask God in prayer and listen for his voice. You can even talk with a trusted friend, counselor, leader, or pastor and listen for God's direction. Remember, God did not design us to go it alone! I'm sure Bertha talked with her friends about Jonah.

Letting go of someone doesn't mean you don't love them, it just means that God is taking over for a little while. God won't let them drown. That is how Bertha found herself in this situation to begin with!

So are you ready to be a whale? Go out, make disciples, and be a light to people around you. Just keep swimming!

Reflection Verses

But I tell you, love your enemies and pray for those who persecute you, that you may be children of your Father in heaven. He causes his sun to rise on the evil and the good, and sends rain on the righteous and the unrighteous.

Matthew 5:44-45

Let us not become weary in doing good, for at the proper time we will reap a harvest if we do not give up. Therefore, as we have opportunity, let us do good to all people, especially to those who belong to the family of believers.

Galatians 6:9-10

"'Love the Lord your God with all your heart and with all your soul and with all your mind and with all your strength.' The second is this: 'Love your neighbor as yourself.' There is no commandment greater than these."

Mark 12:30-31

sixteen

Influencer

Judges 13-16

We've all been told to be careful with whom we keep company. Those of you who went to Sunday school may have heard the cautionary tale of Samson and Delilah, full of best-selling drama. I wish the Bible had more than three chapters on these intriguing characters, but alas, we need to once again read the scripture and put on our creativity hats.

Delilah is a lady of mystery. We know very little about her and her motives, but can see she is a smart and persuasive woman. Samson, the man with a chip on his shoulder, was set apart for God by his parents. Samson was not a man who made wise choices with women. Together, these two make a dynamic duo.

So often in this story I have seen Delilah portrayed as the female villain tricking Samson. Samson is a man that hears from God but has very little discernment. He reminds me of many Christians in today's world. They know the rights and wrongs of the Bible. They know the stories. But their depth of having potential to impact, self-control, discernment, joy, and peace is stuck at a beginner's level.

As Christians, we have the potential to get so much more out of life, yet most of us never go past the beginner level. We are satisfied with apples being our only fruit, when God offers us plenty more fruit in the Bible. God offers us the fruits of the spirit, discernment, and power to change lives through miracles. Is it time for you to go to the next level and ask for more fruit?

Samson had strength beyond a normal man's strength. His impact could have been huge, on the people of Israel and other nations, but Samson lacked something: discernment. I find it to be the single biggest tool that God gives us. It's a tool that needs to sharpened, because if neglected, it can be way off base.

Samson does some cool things recorded in his three chapters. I have always been partial to the story of the foxes being tied together. Yes, the story is sad for the foxes, but the creativity of this act is fascinating. Samson does not seem to do things halfway. Even in his relationship with Delilah, he is all in.

Delilah can easily be blamed for the downfall of Samson. But I think Samson thinking he has everything under control and forgetting where his power comes from is his true downfall. Delilah had Samson's love and his ear. She took advantage of a man who had lost his focus. Delilah's pleas and nagging would not have been as effective if Samson had been listening to God as much as he had been listening to her.

I am guilty of this in my own life (though I am no physical intimidation to others). I am bad at saying "no." The truth is, if I would take the time to see if the ask lines up with the direction I am going instead of thinking about the person I would be disappointing, I would say no more often.

I have said yes to things like doing laundry for other people. Note, I do not do laundry for my family. why in the world would I volunteer to do laundry for others? Yes, I want to help in a real way that helps people. But I have found that working outside of your strengths can cause frustration and resentment in your own life.

For example, if you are dealing with infertility, it may not be in your best interest to volunteer in the nursery. It may feel good to hold babies at the time, but you still go home to an empty house only filled with your tears (personal truth there). I needed to put down the baby and see what plans I should say yes to. When you say yes because you're afraid to say no, you might miss an opportunity that would have been life giving.

Samson said yes to a woman because he lost his focus. After the first time Delilah called in the soldiers to take him away, he should have used his God-given brain to cut ties with her. Delilah may have been beautiful and smart, but Samson was also beautiful and smart. He was chosen by God to be set apart, to speak for God to his people and rule over Israel. Delilah was no mastermind; she continued to believe the crazy schemes Samson would tell her about where his strength came from.

Though Delilah was getting paid to get Samson to give up the secret of his strength, we are not sure if that was her original motive for being with him. She could have loved Samson at one point. Money and influence do crazy things to people.

Delilah was persistent. After the second time he lied about the source of his strength, I would have been too embarrassed to keep going, but not her. I think each time he lied, it drove a wedge between the two of them, making Delilah more determined and Samson more eager to make her happy. Delilah did betray Samson. She sold her love to the people who wanted to kill him. Delilah is not heard from again after his final arrest.

I have always wondered why Samson did not reveal that his strength was from God. Why not lead Delilah to the Lord and show her God's power and love? If Delilah was a woman who knew the Lord, she would have understood that it was not his hair that gave him strength. His hair was merely a representation of promise to set himself apart for God. But Samson did not reveal his connection with God, he only shared the power of his hair.

I feel bad for Delilah. She did not make much money betraying Samson. She could have been a woman of influence at his side, but she used her power to trick and destroy. She listened to the wrong people. I don't think she ever saw the whole picture; Samson ruled over Israel for twelve years and caused terror in the hearts of his enemies, and she only saw a man she could control.

In life, when we let the wrong people influence us we forget to see the whole picture. We have all made mistakes like Samson and Delilah. We need to choose our friends carefully, as well as the things we let influence us: podcasts, social media, music, the list goes on and on. Samson did not take the time to see the influence Delilah was having on his life. I am sure it didn't happen over-night, it was most likely a slow process of trusting her over listening to God.

What people or things have you let drown out the voice of God in your life? Have you placed others' words above the words spoken to you by God through the Bible? Have you stepped into a situation that is over your head and you need God to come in and help?

It is never too late to ask for God's power. It is never too late to listen to his voice. God knows your strengths and weaknesses. He can speak and give you more discernment. This life was not meant to be walked through alone, hoping to find purpose each day. Life was meant to be a daily adventure with God. A life full of purpose and joy. A joy beyond our circumstances.

Reflection Verses

Do not make friends with a hot-tempered person,
    do not associate with one easily angered,
or you may learn their ways
    and get yourself ensnared.

Proverbs 22:24-25

Do not be misled: Bad company corrupts good character.

1 Corinthians 15:33

Iron sharpens iron,
    so a friend sharpens a friend.

Proverbs 27:17 NLT

seventeen

Labeled

Luke 8:40-48

Twelve years! Twelve years is a long time to be sick or to endure anything. The woman in three of the gospels, referred to by the early church as Veronica, endured bleeding for twelve years. I find it interesting that her story is mentioned in three gospels, yet she is never mentioned by name. My guess is so that we focus on the moment she spent with Jesus and not her past.

If the name was good enough for the early church, we are going to refer to her as Veronica as well.

Veronica only has a few paragraphs written about her in the midst of another miracle in progress. Jesus had crossed the sea and was crowded by people. A young ruler came and said his twelve-year-old daughter was dying and she needed Jesus. As Jesus is fighting the crowds to get to the young girl, Veronica plucks up enough courage to touch the hem of Jesus' garment. Veronica is healed.

When Jesus asks who touched him, the disciples say, "Um, *everyone*, Jesus. Do you see this crowd?" Veronica admits her action, Jesus gives her words of encouragement, and just when you think things could not get crazier, a servant comes and says that the young girl is dead. Wow. That is a lot of action in a short period of time.

I have always wondered why Veronica touched the hem of Jesus' clothes and then tried to hide. After 12 years of seeing doctor after doctor, her hope was gone. She was going to be unclean her whole life. She was not supposed to be in a crowd of people. Veronica took a big risk by seeking out Jesus in a crowd; she should have been isolated because of her bleeding.

When we run out of options, we still have the miraculous hem of Jesus to reach for.

Veronica must have endured pain, shame, and loneliness due to a problem that she did not cause. Although I do believe there are natural consequences for sin, I do not believe that every illness is caused by sin. Sometimes you just get sick. Your daughter coughs on you and—boom!—you cough soon, too.

The Bible does not give specifics on her disease or her past, and I think that's why. I think God wants to show that he doesn't care why she got sick, He just wants us to know that He can heal. As Jesus moves on to the young girl, Veronica is interviewed by one of Jesus' followers. Jesus didn't ask about the details of her illness, it's span and what the doctors had to say about it. I love that one of his followers cared enough about her miracle to stop and ask. He was most likely one of the few people in the last 12 years who took time to chat with her and see her as more than a patient or a sinful, unclean woman.

God sees us where we are, too. He sees beyond the things others see. He sees our heart and loves us where and as we are.

This simple act of asking a few questions shows us how we really ought to be as Christ followers. "Man looks at the outer person, but God looks at the heart" (1 Samuel 16:7), is a verse we use to prevent others from judging us. We need to do the same. We need to stop and ask a few questions of those who are struggling before *and* after their miracle comes.

Over 10 years ago, my husband and I took a huge risk as he quit his stable job to go into full-time ministry. His last date of employment was October 31. Why do I remember that date? I remember that date because the next day, as we found ourselves without insurance, I ended up in the ER with my first kidney stone. I remember praying to God to take me home to heaven. The pain was unbelievable.

I did not know that would be the start of a decade of pain. And I mean real pain! I was having kidney stone attacks every three to six months. I saw specialist after specialist. *Drink more water, lose weight, stop losing weight so fast, avoid this, eat that.* I jumped through every hoop they gave me just to make it stop. There was even a stretch where I passed a stone every week.

Kidney stones are not normally life threatening, but they are killers of days or weeks. I made my life function around kidney stones. I went to work with them. I volunteered at church with them. I even made dinner through the pain. I eventually got so good at masking the pain I stopped using drugs to help.

Then one New Year's Eve evening came along. I had made chicken alfredo with homemade sauce and broccoli. After dinner, I turned on a movie for my daughter and went back to bed in extreme pain. I knew it was another stone—you get the signs down after 10 plus years—but this one was different. It had been eight or more years since I had gone to the ER to have a non-passable stone removed. I counted that a blessing in the midst of this pain-filled season. It was 10 p.m., and I knew something was wrong. I asked my husband to drive me to the ER, dropping my daughter with my in-laws just down the road. I ended up staying in the hospital for several days. What they saw on one of my CT scans was strange; the doctor thought it was dye left from 8 years ago, but later found it was a kidney stone that filled my entire kidney.

I had surgery to remove the painful large stone, went home for a day or two, and then headed back to the ER with the worst pain I have ever experienced. Another stone had gotten stuck. A new ultrasound technician was amazed by all the stones in my kidneys. I ended up with an audience to see all my stones. The buzz was electric, they were all so excited about them.

I had to see a new doctor that specialized in large stones. Thankfully, he was able to remove the stone in one surgery, I stayed in the hospital for another five days, and then went home to recover.

The best part of this story is that after the stone removal, my new doctor gave me a new drug that prevents kidney stones! I have had 18 glorious months without a kidney stone attack. That is a miracle!

Veronica had suffered for so long that she knew no different. The only thing she knew to do was to sneak around and hope that the rumors of Jesus were true. Jesus healed people; why not her? And why not you?

No matter the shame, no matter the illness, no matter the pain, Jesus can heal you. Though things may seem hopeless and painful, the pain may lead you to your answer. Without that last attack on New Year's Eve, I may not have found the answer to end my constant pain.

God can use your pain to get you to your miracle. Veronica faced punishment in order to seek her miracle, and she was greatly rewarded for her faith. The 12-year-old girl's miracle was postponed as Jesus fought through the crowds to get to her; she died. The miracle still came when Jesus raised her from the dead.

God doesn't work in our timing. He may be healing that someone scared to be seen in the crowd as He is on his way to heal you. We just need to keep seeking Jesus. His miraculous touch is still available for you today. Yours may be a simple miracle of making the stone pass faster or a miracle of enduring the worst pain of your life to discover the solution to your pain. God has a plan for your miracle; keep seeking after Jesus' hem.

Reflection Verses

Ask and it will be given to you; seek and you will find;
knock and the door will be opened to you.

Matthew 7:7

Trust in the Lord with all your heart
    and lean not on your own understanding;
in all your ways submit to him,
    and he will make your paths straight.

Proverbs 3:5-6

eighteen

Loved One

Genesis 29 -30

Rachel came from a family of sheepherders and was so beautiful that a man fell in love with her at first sight. I cannot even imagine her beauty in a field full of smelly sheep. Jacob worked for 14 years to gain her as his wife, so she must have been more than beautiful to inspire that kind of dedication. Also important to note: she was the second daughter of Jacob's mom's relative.

As we look into Rachel's story, we must remember that her life, like her sister Leah's, was dictated by men. She did make choices in the life she was handed, but she did not have the choices and options we all have today. Rachel did not decide to complicate life by sharing her husband with her sister. If I had to guess, she was not happy about the arrangement.

Not only did Rachel have to share her husband, but really, she had to share her wedding. Leah needed to be married and this need became a cost Rachel had to pay. Jacob loved Rachel, and I am sure she was excited about the wedding, but to have your dad sabotage the whole thing? Frustrating, to say the least.

And then—to make matters worse—your sister, who has already stolen your wedding night, starts popping out babies. And not only babies, but BOYS! Rachel must have been miserable. Yes, she had Jacob's love and affection, but she did not feel she had the Lord's favor.

Quite often, life seems perfect from the outside. Rachel was beautiful and loved by Jacob. They were prosperous with lots of healthy sheep. How could life be any more perfect?

We know that what we see is not always the truth. Someone in your life may seem to be living the high life, traveling the world, doing things you have always wanted to do…and likely posting it all over social media. We have no idea what they may be dealing with behind the scenes.

Many years ago my family was on a long road trip to Maine. We were traveling for ministry (preaching at churches along the way) and staying at less than fancy hotels. We ate picnics of peanut butter sandwiches every lunch at wayside stops. Although we had a very tight budget, I planned theme days. I packed outfits for my young daughter to wear, like a tutu, to have ballerina day. When we stopped for lunch, we danced and ate our lunch. We read books and played games that went with the theme of the day. We stopped at every free attraction we could find. It was a blast. And it was on this trip that we decided traveling would become a family priority.

I remember getting grief from a friend when we returned from that trip. They said that their family could never afford that kind of trip, mentioning that their extra money goes toward missions. I was so upset. We had been so conservative on that trip, even staying in a pastor's home for a few days to save money, but all my friends saw was a trip across the country and our good life.

Since making travel a family priority, we make daily sacrifices to travel. We live in a trailer, we do not eat out much, and we almost always buy generic, all so we can travel. We use hotel and airline points, and yet so many say, "We wish we could travel like you do, it must be nice." First, if you want help on how to travel cheap, contact me. I have lots of advice. Second, no one sees the sacrifice, they only see the reward.

This idea applies to your life as well. Many only see the promotion, not the hard work you put in to get it. Our jealousy of others' successes is just a way to remind ourselves that life is not all it appears to be. God can shine on you as well as your neighbors.

Rachel is very unhappy and yells at Jacob for not giving her a baby. She is only able to see Leah's babies, blind to Leah's misery in not being loved. I would guess both women would have traded spots to have what the other had, but would have realized that the grass is not always greener on the other side.

Comparing your life to others' is not a healthy way to live. I could look at my friends' beautiful homes and get jealous of "all" they have. Then I remind myself that is the way they choose to spend their money, and I choose to travel. Some people seem to have it all, yet we do not know what their finances look like or what they have sacrificed to get all those things. Do not compare yourself to others' outward appearances.

It's time to take a look at the blessings God has given you. Take some time to think about the things you are jealous of in someone else's life (can't think of anything? scroll through social media!), and then make a column of God's blessings to you in that area. What do you need to give to God?

Fast forward in time…way too long of a time for Rachel…and she's done everything she knows how to do on her own to have a child. She has given her maidservant to her husband for marriage. She bought mandrakes (a fertility booster) from her sister in exchange for time with her husband, and Rachel is still childless.

Rachel sees that without God, a child would not be possible. We often take for granted the things in life that others struggle with, like having children. But when we struggle with them ourselves, it is clear to see God's hand moving in that area.

If you keep reading about Jacob, you will see that Rachel struggles with God providing in other areas, too. She steals the idols from her father's home when they leave to start on their own. Did she need the idols or was she unsure if God was in the move? We can only guess. But this act leads to several lies—her sin is compounding! We rarely sin just once; we often need to sin several times to keep the original sin a secret.

Though Rachel may have been the favorite, she spent most of her life playing the comparison game. She was the mother to Joseph, who saved his family, and he was Jacob's favorite. Joseph was highly favored by God, yet not liked by his brothers. The comparison trap fell to the next generation, between Joseph's brothers, which led to a moment in time where they almost killed Joseph. But God had different plans. God took this jealousy and used it to save Egypt.

Rachel was not perfect. Her life was not perfect. God's plan for her son was not easy. When you look at her life, she had it all and it was never enough. Her sons made a big impact in the world. And though she never changed the world herself, she could have with her influence. But I believe her lack of self-esteem held her back from being the influencer she could have been to her family. I think we all need to learn this from Rachel's story: *being you is enough.*

Believe in yourself. God believes in you. He has plans for you. If you do not believe me, take some time to research "plans for you" in the Bible. Read the verses about being knit together in the womb by God. These verses are about *you*! The truth will be life-changing if you let the love of the Lord and his plans for you sink into your heart.

Reflection Verses

For you created my inmost being;
    you knit me together in my mother's womb.
I praise you because I am fearfully and wonderfully
      made;
    your works are wonderful, I know that full well.

Psalm 139:13-14

We can make our plans,
    but the LORD determines our steps..

Proverbs 16:9 NLT

And the very hairs on your head are all numbered. So don't be afraid; you are more valuable to God than a whole flock of sparrows.

Luke 12:7 NLT

nineteen

Cornered Cat

Job 1-2

I have been fascinated with Job since I was in sixth grade, when I had to pick a Bible story to write a report about for reading class at my small private school. I should have chosen a short story, since we were required to read it three times. Yet this stubborn sixth grader insisted that Job had too much to teach me to *not* make it my project.

I do not remember the project. In fact, I am sure like many of my projects that year, I got a ketchup bottle on my desk (for when you had work that was late and you needed to "ketchup") due to not completing the writing portion of the project. I also remember writing down many verses from Job and slipping them places where my parents they may find them, in an effort to encourage them in whatever was making my mom cry at night when she thought we couldn't hear her.

We meet Job and his family in the prime of life. He has riches, livestock, lots of children, and favor with God. This sets his story apart from the get-go. We usually hear the problems first. Job is faithful to God and looks to Him for guidance in this time of his life.

We see the back-story where Satan comes to God and says that Job is only faithful because of the blessings given to him. God grants Satan the ability to take away the things Job holds dear.

Job's world crashes. He loses his children, livestock, and health. He is a mess, but Job still praises God. Really, when you think about it, what else does he have left? God was his source of joy before the tragedies, and he now needed God more than before.

Not everyone in Job's life agrees with this logic. He has three friends that spend most of the book of Job trying to convince him to give up. To me, the most interesting person in this story has no name and is mentioned once. Job's wife! She has one line, "Are you still holding on to your integrity? Curse God and die!"

Job's wife tells her husband, please die. She was not even polite. That is certainly not how I would want to be remembered.

I want to take a minute and look at this story, their situation, from her eyes. She lost everything alongside Job. She was most likely with him when the servant came to tell them that all their children had died. That alone would tip anyone into depression. But to watch your servants die, livestock die, and now your husband is on death's door? It's too much loss for anyone! She must have been hopeless. Job was a great man of faith, he saw the whole picture, but I think she only saw her pain. Her pain must have been so great that she wanted to give up. She wanted Job to give up. She had no hope, and she just wanted to make the pain stop.

We all do lots of things to make the pain stop. One of those is yelling. When we are in pain we lash out at people we love, people driving too slow, people at the store, and the list could go on and on. When we are in pain, we sometimes act like a cornered cat. I think Job's wife is a cornered cat here, she does not know what to do with her pain. She sees things getting worse and worse. And just when she thought she had hit rock bottom, the bottom was crushed into gravel and she fell further. I am sure she had to have been thinking, *What else can happen?*

And though a cornered cat she may be, she does have some valuable lessons to teach us. First, and for me the hardest, is to keep our mouths shut. One of my favorite verses (as I have said before) is Proverbs 17:28: "Even a fool who keeps silent is considered wise; when he closes his lips, he is deemed intelligent." If she would have taken her thoughts about Job to God in prayer instead of cursing him and asking him to die, she may have understood where her husband got his faith. Maybe not, but it would have been better to have been the woman who cried out to God than the wife who was rebuked by her husband.

Another good lesson for those of us who try to use our words to fix a problem: our words cannot be taken back. We were really just trying to help, or sharing how we feel. Words can cut deep. May we be remembered for our wise silence, not our foolish advice.

And a third lesson we can take from this story is that it's hard to be thankful for God's blessings and angry when pain comes. My husband has been keeping a thankful journal for twenty plus years. Every night, he writes five things that he is thankful for from that day. His journals have become a timeline for him and a daily reminder of God's blessings, though some days it's hard to come up with five things to be thankful for.

I've tried to do thankful journals but lose the journal after a week, start a new one, find the old one, and make a grocery list in it. And the cycle continues. I do have other ways of taking time to see God's blessings, just none that take organization like the one where you fill a jar with a blessing a day to open on New Year's Eve. Great idea, though mine would be full of January and December, with one or two from the days I moved the jar for dusting. My reminders are more simple, like a question I ask my daughter every day, "How was your day? Tell me your favorite part."

We all have trials in life. We all have days that we see others struggle and wonder why they don't just give up and try something else. We want what is best for the ones we love and for ourselves, and we often equate that with what is easiest. I have had days where getting out of bed seemed impossible both physically and emotionally.

So what keeps me going? HOPE! I believe God's plan for me is not to sit in the past. He has bigger things in store for me. God restores Job's wealth, health and gives him more children (though of course, they didn't replace the ones he lost). God shows us through Job's story that even when you are at your lowest, God sees you and has a plan to renew you.

Hold on to hope. Start some thankful routines in your life. Ask God to show you his plan and his love for you. Do not give up on Him!

Reflection Verse

Even a fool who keeps silent is considered wise;
    when he closes his lips, he is deemed intelligent

Proverbs 17:28 ESV

Always be joyful. Never stop praying. Be thankful in all circumstances, for this is God's will for you who belong to Christ Jesus.

1 Thessalonians 5:16-18 NLT

twenty

Peace Maker

1 Samuel 25 1:44

We meet lots of interesting characters in the book of Samuel, yet my favorite might just be Abigail. She is described as intelligent and beautiful. We meet Abigail as she is helping an outlaw of the land. Her husband, Nabal, is said to be a mean evildoer. Their pairing seems a little Beauty and the Beast to me. Nabal is rude, without manners, and short sighted. On the other hand, Abigail seems to see the big picture of situations.

After David has the opportunity to kill Saul, he flees to the area of Carmel. David and his men are running low on supplies, so it's time to make some deals. David's men have been looking after the servants in a field that belongs to Nabal. When David sends servants to Nabal to negotiate for what they need after doing him a good service, Nabal rudely says no! David's men had helped Nabal's men, but no kindness was returned. Nabal has made a couple of mistakes here.

First, Nabal underestimated David's pride and temper. I do not think Nabal was necessarily wrong in saying no to "repay" David's men. Short-sighted, maybe. He didn't see the potential for trouble. David was on the run from the king of Israel; he's an outlaw at this time in history. You don't want to be seen giving Robin Hood supplies if you think the sheriff will find out. Since Nabal didn't know David's full story, he didn't know that David doesn't like to be told no. He will fight that giant if he wants to! If you look at David's life, there's definitely a pattern of him not listening to no's.

Secondly, Nabal underestimated David's support system. Since David only sent ten men to ask for supplies, Nabal was foolish to not seek the details that would paint the full picture of the force on David's side. And not only the men with him, but the God David served. Nabal underestimated God. He foolishly called the servants names and didn't even allow them to get water.

The Bible is harsh with Nabal. Mostly, Nabal's is a story of not being generous. It's easy to be generous when you feel you have plenty and that God will continue to supply for your needs. We don't know why Nabal was so cranky with the servants, other than he likely saw a bunch of vagabonds trying to take advantage of his wealth. For me, this is a wakeup call. Do I really believe my resources come from God? If I truly believe that the God who made the earth and the stars supplies my needs, then why am I not giving more freely?

As all of this mess is going on the servants start to panic. They have good reason. They have spent time with David, they know his personality, and they know his army. They run to Abigail. I love the respect she must have had from her maids and the others who served her household. They would never have run to a wife that they didn't respect or thought would cower in fear of her husband. Abigail acts quickly, not fearful of her husband's actions.

110

As she makes plans, David is making some of his own. Abigail is trying to save her home, her husband is getting ready to celebrate the shearing of the sheep, and David is getting ready for a fight. There's so much drama going on and Nabal is completely ignorant of everything around him.

With her authority, Abigail sends food and wine ahead of her to meet David and his men. Their wealth must have been great to have all the food she sent David, with plenty left over for the party her husband was having. The cooks must have been crazy busy! Two hundred loaves of bread would wipe out an Aldi's entire bread section today.

Abigail arrives after the food. She isn't a fool. This woman knows not to come empty handed to an angry mob of men, and she arrived after the provisions in hopes they are no longer "hangry" (hungry *and* angry). Abigail arrives and throws herself at the mercy of David. She explains her husband's folly and begs for forgiveness.

Here is where her intelligence comes to play. She knows her husband's actions are not something that David is going to overlook just because his wife asks for mercy. David wants Nabal to admit that he was rude and insulting. So Abigail turns this situation into a plea to save David's reputation. Abigail's boldness is impressive, but not enough to make David's anger subside. Seeing the food, wine, and groveling is not going to be enough, Abigail pulls out the big guns. She convinces David that she is sparing David from committing murder, not vengeance. He should not want the rumors of this murder to reach others' ears; he should want the act of kindness to go ahead of him.

Abigail has David's attention. A beautiful woman comes out to save her home, and now she's trying to save him, too. This is some special woman. Surely, Abigail was sent by God to keep David from spilling innocent blood.

After risking her life to save her home and family, Abigail comes home to a very wild party. Nabal is very drunk, not even able to hear her story. When he is sober enough to listen to Abigail's tale, he is so afraid he stops moving and soon dies. How was Abigail so brave and her husband such a fraidy cat?

As soon as David hears of Nabal's death, he sends for Abigail and makes her his second wife. The story for Abigail is just beginning. Now she is David's wife. A man being hunted by the king. It's a good thing she has nerves of steel; she's going to need them!

Abigail goes from being married to a foolish and evil-doing man, to a man who is running and fighting for his life. David will eventually become king, but in the meantime, Abigail and the third wife are taken prisoner. David is on one of his campaigns when a group of people comes and takes everything he has, including his two wives. They are rescued, but things are weird for Abigail the rest of her married life.

Of course, Abigail had to share David with his other wives, but when he took Bathsheba the betrayal must have been deep. David was not content with what he had in life. The night he took Bathsheba, Abigail learned she was just a prop in someone else's life. She was a brave woman who feared the Lord, and she never got the respect she fully deserved.

There are times in life when we take risks for others and get no thanks for our actions. We can also feel like an afterthought in someone else's story. God sees us behind the others in the picture. Or for me, he sees me behind the camera. God had a plan to use Abigail to save many people, including David from himself. Her bravery is easily forgotten by many, but not by God.

God sees you hiding behind that camera. He sees your need to be loved and cherished, not because of duty but for who you are. God sees your potential for greatness. Abigail's act of bravery and quick thinking really did save many, but mostly it gave her the opportunity to influence a king and his wives. David may not have cherished her later, but she would have been a leader among his many wives. God placed an intelligent, caring, and compassionate woman in David's home to advise and nurture the other wives and to make sure the kingdom God was building ran smoothly. She kept God first, not destroying David with the distraction of drama and other gods to worship. I am sure she kept a strict house and always knew what was happening.

You may think your role in life is small or insignificant. God needs you to be with those toddlers, keeping chaos to a simmer. God has put you in a place of honor. Just look around you and see your influence.

We all need a reminder of our purpose. For me, it's keeping the faith in my little family that when we all want to give up, God still has a plan. I think God uses us when we insert a joke that lightens the mood or say a silent prayer. God has placed us there, in that moment, for His works. God has placed you in your work, church, and family for just this time. God has given you talents and perspective that only you can use to make a difference in the situations around you.

Reflection Verse

"For if you remain silent at this time, relief and deliverance for the Jews will arise from another place, but you and your father's family will perish. And who knows but that you have come to your royal position for such a time as this?"

Esther 4:14

twenty-one

Salty One

Genesis 19

"Remember Lot's wife! Whoever tries to keep their life will lose it, and whoever loses their life will preserve it" (Luke 17:32-33). Jesus spoke these words many years after the story of Lot's wife. Hers is a story we consider a "follow Jesus and do not look back" tale. Though she's never named and we know very little about her, I think we can learn so much from this interesting woman.

We know that she is from Sodom and that Lot married her after he split from Abraham. Lot and Abraham started their journey to follow the Lord's word and find a new land together. They didn't plan to do their own thing. From day one their plan was to adventure through life *together*. Famine forced them into Egypt, and then they returned to Canaan where the fighting got bad. Their shepherds were fighting; at this point, we see both men had wealth. They each have enough livestock that the people working for them are fighting over where to graze the animals. I know nothing about grazing animals, but I do know that there are never enough swings at the park. One child is always left pushing. As every parent knows, quarreling children can drive you crazy. Abraham had enough. He gave Lot the choice of land. That was a big choice: playground or sandbox. Lot chose the playground, the land that looked best and seemed more fun.

This new land is where he finds his wife. And while it may or may not have been related to finding his wife, he winds up needing to be rescued. The king of Sodom takes all of his stuff and Abraham has to rescue him, his stuff, and his family.

We see no evidence that Lot's wife followed God the way he did. Lot and his wife tent outside the city of Sodom; his tent faced the town. This shows how much influence his wife had in their home.

When we're young, we don't get to choose our friends. They are our neighbors, schoolmates, and the kids of our parents' friends. Those influences are chosen for us. My parents loved to entertain, so I was surrounded by lots of different kids. We had people over all the time; when I was six, they even had boys over and I was not thrilled. My friends were the people that were around, my school friends lived far away so the boys of my parents' friends were who I spent my time with. To be fair, the boys did get me out of my shell by teaching me how to dive off my desk, on to my waterbed, and crash without making enough noise for my parents to hear. But the main thing I learned from those boys was that they liked to be crazy and enjoyed seeing me fly through the air.

In seventh grade everything changed. I had choices. It was not easy to choose to move away from friends that were comfortable to find new friends with my interests. One close friend that I chose to pull away from was a church friend who became interested in boys with bad reputations. I wanted friends seeking after God's heart, and she was looking for something different. My new friends may not have seemed as cool as her new friends, but I felt mine would lead me down a better path.

About eight months after this division of friendship, we remained "friends," we just didn't hang out much anymore. Throughout life we've stayed in touch, but we have gone down very different paths. Hers was filled with horrors and pain. Bad boys do bad things. And while my life has not been perfect, I have said to my husband many times that the choices I made in seventh grade kept me from lots of pain.

Lot's wife was not a good influence in his life. He stayed in the city that stole everything from him, just to please her. The town they lived in was full of sin, so much so that the Lord wanted to destroy it.

Let's collectively scream together: *"Run, Lot. RUN!"*

To be blunt, this lady is not my favorite. She has no faith and seems to be a terrible influence on her family. Is this her fault or the culture's? I'm not sure. As I'm sure you've gathered by this point, Lot's wife is not someone we want to make our hero, but we should want to learn from her mistakes.

When angels come to Sodom to rescue Lot, we're given a glimpse of why the Lord wanted to destroy the city. Lot is given the chance to save his extended family and the men pledged to his two daughters. He tells the men to flee the city with his daughters because the Lord is about to destroy it, and they think he's joking.

If Lot's wife had been taking the threat seriously, her daughters may have as well and pleaded with their fiancés to reconsider. Her unbelief not only took her life, but it took the life of her extended family. None of them fled the city. It's honestly surprising she left with Lot and the angels.

As they reach the city for safety, Lot's wife looks back at Sodom against the angels' direction and turns to a pillar of salt. Quite the punishment for a glance. Was it punishment for the look or her desire to stay in her sinful life? Only God really knows. From what we see in the story, it seems that she didn't want to leave her home or family. She didn't speak up to save her two daughters from the men of Sodom, she let Lot take them on, and ultimately the Lord saved them all that evening. I'm not saying she should have done anything crazy, but perhaps her punishment covered more than the glance.

A pillar of salt standing where your mom once stood would shake anyone to his or her core. Afraid to stay in that place, Lot and his daughters fled to the mountains. I've never fully understood this call, because Lot tells the angels earlier that going to the mountains would destroy him. Maybe this post pillar-of-salt call would ensure that none of them looked back as well. I believe the look was not the main reason she was punished. It was her heart that longed for the look. Her look was no mistake, it was an action indicating how she longed for Sodom. Lot fleeing to the mountains was most likely an effort to be sure his girls didn't try to look back as well.

Lot's wife wasn't ready to give up her old life to look forward to the new promises that God had for her. In our lives, it's easy to look back and long for the comfort of our old life and old choices. But God has new paths for you. If you spend your time day dreaming about the good old days, you may miss the good *new* days. Keep your remembrances short, and with an eye on the promises God has for you today.

Is it time to let go of the past and reach for new goals? What do you need to let go of in order to move forward?

Reflection Verses

I will lead the blind by ways they have not known,
    along unfamiliar paths I will guide them;
I will turn the darkness into light before them
    and make the rough places smooth.
These are the things I will do;
    I will not forsake them.

Isaiah 42:16

See, I am doing a new thing!
    Now it springs up; do you not perceive it?
I am making a way in the wilderness
    and streams in the wasteland.

Isaiah 43:19

twenty-two

The Unnamed Zookeeper

Genesis 6-9

When you think about trials in the Bible, we often think of Daniel and the lions, Israel wondering in the desert, the many battles in the Old Testament, the list could go on and on. But until I read it the other day, I had never really thought of the flood as a trial or tragedy. It is hard to see bad in something that produced the world's first rainbow.

My daughter's favorite saying is "You cannot have a rainbow without the rain." Wisdom for us all.

As we take a look at the building of the ark in Genesis, I want you to put your imagination hat back on your head. Noah is called by God to build an ark and is given very specific instructions for how to build this big boat.

Let's just pause here. I cannot even imagine my husband coming home and saying, "I have a new project. I am building a huge boat." Now, while he has come up with "you must be out of your mind" ideas, my husband has never suggested a building project that would save the world. But to be honest, I have sometimes felt his ideas came close to this "build a big boat" plan.

Imagine how Noah's wife must have felt when he shared God's plan with her. Going from personal experience, it may have gone something like, "That's nice dear, I am sure God has a plan?" Or, "Noah, you must have heard wrong. You are no carpenter and that blueprint sounds too big to accomplish." Maybe the question of, "And how do you suppose we'll pay for this big boat?" With an added, "What will our friends think?" I'm not sure what my exact reaction would have been, but I certainly would have said, *"We can do this if God gives me a sign!"*

But the ark is not the extent of the plan. Next comes the part about two of each creature. "Noah, you cannot mean that God wants you to save the spiders and then put ME on a boat with them?" "I will not be helping with the crocodiles, they are dangerous. And do not get me started on the howler monkeys!"

And as we read on in their story, we see the people turned on Noah (and his family). "Noah, enough! I'm losing my friends because of your crazy idea, it's time to stop this now."

Noah's wife is never named, and only mentioned once in the Bible. She must have been overwhelmed by the frustration of her life taking such a sharp turn because of what God tells her husband to do. There's no record in the Bible of her complaining or arguing, or helping for that matter. She had to have been supportive or Noah likely would never have finished his mission for God. I could be wrong. Maybe he had to hog tie her and place her on the boat. I believe she is like a lot of us: she saw God's dream planted in someone, had doubts and voiced them, then meets with God and finally supports the crazy boat plan. And when the animal plan came, repeated the process.

She was on the boat and endured the forty days of rain, and then it was almost a full year before she got off this smelly, miraculous boat. In this time she may have often cried, "Why God?" She may have screamed over the howler monkeys, "Noah, I am so angry with you for getting into this situation." And I bet she praised God for saving her and her family.

I call this the rollercoaster of faith. God does not expect us to just go with the flow and never speak up. He's tough enough to hear our rollercoaster of emotions, and actually wants us to take those to him.

The Bible says "cast all your cares on him" (1 Peter 5:7). This implies we have cares and worries. We're not expected to be perfect, but we are expected to daily (sometimes hourly) give all our cares and worries to him.

As we look at Noah's wife, we can only imagine what her daily (hourly) prayers were. God may have known her as well as Noah, yet my guess is that you've never really given her a second thought. She went through the same trials as Noah. She lost friends and family in the flood. She helped take care of an ark full of fun and scary creatures.

In my life, I live in the shadow of a Godly man who is doing great things around the country. I do not get recognized when we are shopping or even after service. Many simply know me as Kevin's wife. I have both reveled in the anonymity and felt left out. I have cried out, "God, I want to make a difference," on my rollercoaster of faith. I often doubt God before the miracle comes, and think he's saving the big jobs for the pastors and missionaries. I sometimes feel like they're called to do cool stuff while I'm gliding along in life with no purpose.

I imagine that Noah's wife had her doubts, yet fully trusted God. Can doubts and trust coexist in a situation?

In July of 2005, my husband and I sat chatting about our next step. Our church plant of eight years was struggling with nine people attending (six of those being our family). The church experienced great success in the past, but here we were chatting about closing the church. Where was God? We had followed him into this church plant and poured our hearts into the people and city. Here we stood, mostly alone. We lost friends. We tried to build something that we had felt God had given us the blueprint to build, and it had failed. I will never forget the day I changed our voicemail to a non-church recording (in fact, my husband still uses that recording). I was heartbroken and confused. I had prayed and followed the steps I felt we were given. My rollercoaster of faith was in full swing.

Soon my husband was excited for our next chapter: traveling to encourage pastors and teaching on prayer. I saw no place for me in that vision. I asked the same questions I imagine Noah's wife had. "Is this a good plan?" "How are we going to make money?" And of course, "God give me a sign." It seemed like a bad plan. Were we just jumping into another failure? We built an ark, it sank, and now my husband wants to try it again but with a slightly different blueprint.

We have no idea how many times Noah misread the instructions for building the ark. How many nails did he pull out? How many days did he come home defeated? All we know is that he succeeded. Noah's wife was there through it all. The days he doubted himself, the days he doubted he heard right.

What blueprint is God giving you? I have a reminder on my wall at work that quotes Psalm 121, "Where does my help come from?" I often find myself not doubting God's ability, but mine. He is my support. He knows my name. He knew Noah's wife's name. God believed she was the right person to stand beside Noah when he gave him this huge assignment. Together, they helped the world start over. She was a strength to her husband, her sons and daughter-in-laws. I believe her strength came from the same God that gave her husband the blueprint to save the world. She was not a sidekick. God needed her to make a difference, even if the world would never know her name.

Reflection Verse

Let the morning bring me word of your unfailing love,
    for I have put my trust in you.
Show me the way I should go,
    for to you I entrust my life.

Psalm 143:8

twenty-three

Behind the Scenes Benefactor

Luke 8:1-3; Mark 16

If you take nothing else from these stories, I want you to know that God uses broken and sinful people. Mary Magdalene was one of the most broken. Her choices in life before Jesus are far from ideal, and her mental stability was compromised by the demons inside her. Really, life was not good for our friend Mary M.

We do not know much about her past. We know nothing about her family. We only know she was free to roam around the country, following Jesus.

Mary M is mentioned fourteen times in the Bible. When mentioned alongside other women, she is mostly named first. She was a leader among the women Jesus healed. Some even think she was part of the day of Pentecost in Acts.

Diving into what's recorded of Mary M's life in the Bible, my thoughts of her changed dramatically. First, I always thought she was a prostitute, but when I looked her up in the Bible, I found no written record of that profession. The only thing I could find mentioning this theory was on the Internet, and you know everything on the Internet is true. The Internet said that the prostitute description was added to her story after the fact. I was shocked. I have heard about her my whole life, but what I learned in church was not fully accurate. I suddenly felt lost in writing about her, until I kept reading in the Bible.

Second, I have always thought she was the Mary who poured a year's wages of perfume on Jesus' feet, cleaning them with her hair and tears. As this Mary (who as I understand now is Mary of Bethany, Lazarus's sister) repents her sins, Judas complains about the waste of money. It's seriously one of my favorite passages in the Bible; I so would have said, "Wow that was a waste! I could have stocked a food shelf with that money." I understand where Judas was coming from. It's hard to see money "wasted" on things you're not passionate about.

Several years ago I decided that if we wanted our daughter to learn to have a generous spirit, we needed to display generosity. When she was little, we started with an Operation Christmas Child box. If you're not aware of this organization, Google it! We gave her the opportunity to shop for a girl her age in another country for Christmas. I remember the thrill she had buying a doll, a jump rope, and a couple of cute hair bows for a girl she would never meet. We still fill boxes every fall to ship to children in need around the world.

Generosity grows. As a family, we've had the opportunity to save money in order to give goats and chickens to people in need around the world. We also love to find missionaries to support, even if it's in small ways. We believe in being generous even when our finances are not good. Our daughter has taken the lessons we've taught her to new levels! At the age of 11, she started raising money by mowing lawns, selling caramel corn, plants, and more to make a difference in missions.

What can you do with what God has given you? Take a moment to thank the Lord for the times he has used others to bless you. When you live life like money is not yours, it is easier to both give it away and to receive. In addition to finances, you can give of your talents as well. What is God laying on your heart to give?

Since my assumptions of Mary M were incorrect, I was surprised that what I found out about her was even better. She was a supporter and follower of Jesus. She was one of the women who dedicated her life to Jesus after being healed from her evil spirits.

Mary M's healing is mentioned so briefly that if you're not looking for it, you may miss it. She had seven demons come out of her. One is pesky, but seven could make you crazy. Two other women are mentioned in this short text: Susanna from Herod's household, and Joanna, wife of Cuza, a steward of Herod. Mary ran with some important company.

The book of Luke goes on to note that these women had money and influence. Knowing this, we know Herod would have had known of Jesus years before Jesus stood in front of him. In Luke 23, we see Herod excited to see Jesus and hoping for a miracle at the trial because of the stories he had heard.

Mary M's healing from seven demons is mentioned like it was an everyday occurrence on the road with Jesus. It may have been an everyday thing for those who were following Jesus, but it wasn't for Mary M. Her life was forever changed the day Jesus set her free.

We see very little of Mary M as the months fade into years of following Jesus. Very few times do we see just the twelve disciples plus Jesus. For all we know, Mary M and the other ladies might have followed alongside them since their release from demons is recorded quickly after the twelve disciples were called.

Mary M's love for Jesus is evident in her generosity and loyalty until the end. We see her with Mary, the mother of Jesus, at the cross. Mary M was there when Jesus died. I imagine she held her friend Mary's hand as they watched the soldiers torture her son. They cried in agony when Jesus was stabbed with a spear. The sight of a crucifixion was not for the faint of heart even when you did not know the victim, but to watch a man you had devoted your life to—your savior—be crucified would have been beyond words. The sights these women saw that day are something only seen in nightmares. Their devotion to Jesus was unwavering. Mary and Mary M stood in the angry crowd and supported Jesus until the very end.

Mary M was strong. She stood in support not only for Jesus, but for his mom as well. It is no accident we hear her name at the cross. I think her being with Mary, mother of Jesus, at the cross provided her with some protection. Mary M had powerful friends!

Mary M is recorded in all four gospels as going to the tomb to prepare Jesus' body for burial. Her tears of frustration and grief at the tomb are not easily forgotten. When the women found the empty tomb, they did not immediately think "Jesus is risen." They had witnessed horrors days before and could not imagine them stopping any time soon. From my understanding, many of Jesus' followers were hiding for fear of being captured and killed themselves. These brave women went out to the tomb to find that their worst thoughts had come true: soldiers had taken Jesus' body to use as an example elsewhere. Their hopelessness was magnified when they found the empty tomb.

We often sit at an empty tomb wondering how life can get any worse. *My situation was bad yesterday, and now this? Why God?* I would like to remind you that the empty tomb may just be the miracle you've been waiting for. You may not see Jesus or hear his directive to go proclaim his victory. You may only see the empty tomb. Know that God's empty tomb is a stepping stone to victory in your life.

God did not leave the women in a place of mourning.

God did not leave the women in a place of fear.

God did not leave the women in a place of confusion.

God gave them Jesus. God gave them victory over death.

How much bigger does he need to be for us to trust him?

Reflection Verse

The LORD is my rock, my fortress, and my savior;
    my God is my rock, in whom I find protection.
He is my shield, the power that saves me,
    and my place of safety.

Psalm 18:2 NLT

twenty-four

Down to Earth Momma

Genesis 2-4

When you hear the name Eve, what pops into your head? A snake? An apple? We are all too familiar with her story: the first woman, Adam's help mate, a friend of God's in the garden of Eden, and then she talks to a snake and becomes the world's first sinner. In the first chapters of the Bible, she racks up quite the resume and is blamed for lots of our sins' consequences. I am grateful she sinned right away. I would hate to have been the person that, after thousands and thousands of years in paradise with God, listened to a snake and ruined it for all mankind. When I get to heaven I will give her a hug and say thank you for taking one for the team, it would have been me later.

Eve starts out in a perfect scenario. Adam is lonely, so God creates Eve. A perfect woman, arguably the most beautiful woman ever created. She is loved by Adam and walks with God in paradise. In the New Testament, Paul writes, "I am afraid that as the serpent deceived Eve by its cunning, your thoughts will be led astray from a sincere and pure devotion to Christ" (2 Cor. 11:3). Of course Eve is deceived, she never had to think about whom she should trust. Her life is perfect, without deception and shame. Up until the serpent joins the story, Eve has only had people in her life who love her and want what is best for her. God is walking with her and showing her unconditional love, and Adam knows no different either. I think we need to give her more grace for listening to a serpent. Her experience with deception was non-existent. We trust until we are wronged.

I like to imagine that Adam and Eve were having a lovely picnic by a waterfall when she shared her forbidden fruit with Adam. The key to the story is that they both disobeyed. In our house, we have taught our daughter that disobedience is doing something you know is wrong. Disobedience is not accidently doing something wrong, it is knowing the rule and choosing to ignore the rule. They both chose to eat the fruit. And *boom!* Shame entered the world for the first time.

Yes, sin entered the world too, but their first act after the sin was to realize they were naked. My guess is that before sin, they just enjoyed being naked. Just like I like to run through the grass barefoot. Being naked was normal to them, but sin came in with shame right on its heels saying, "Cover up your ugliness, no one wants to see that." The ugliness was in their sin, not their bodies. Remember, they were made in God's image and most likely the most perfectly beautiful people ever to live. The shame was not in who they were but in what they had done. They were unable to see the difference. Sin came in and destroyed their self worth with one bite of fruit.

Oxford defines shame as "a painful feeling of humiliation or distress caused by the consciousness of wrong or foolish behavior." Some of us wear shame like a blanket, so wrapped up in it that we do not even see it's there. Honestly, I cannot even imagine living a life without shame. My shame hasn't come from eating forbidden fruit, more like a forbidden donut. Why is this our daily struggle?

How do you know if shame is in your life? Examine your self-talk. Take a week and write down the things you say to yourself in the morning, after a cookie, at work, after a conversation with a coworker or boss, at bedtime, after you made your teen cry. The list could go on and on. Really, just examine what your inner voice is saying. I was embarrassed to write down some of the things that I say to myself. I would be so upset if I ever said any of them to anyone, and devastated if anyone said them to me. I justify them by saying it's just truth or self-discipline.

Here are some examples, and please note that I am not very nice to myself!

"Good morning fatty."

"You are not worthy of love."

"Dumb, dumb, dumb."

If I were brave, I would share more of myself with you, but hopefully now you know that you are not alone. Second Corinthians 10:5 tells us to take captive every thought and make it obedient to Christ. Shame and sin go hand in hand, but Christ died on the cross to defeat them.

You can live in freedom from both. We will never be perfect like Eve was in the garden, but she did not have the blood of Christ to be her new fig leaves. It is a daily (or for me, hourly) process of taking my thoughts captive, giving them to the Lord, and comparing them to what the Bible says about what I am struggling with today.

Do not let the current situation or struggle define who you are in the future. Let the Lord's promises in his word be what defines your future.

Eve's problems only began after eating the fruit. She lost her home, she struggled in having the same closeness with God due to shame and sin, she had less time to spend with Adam (he had to work the land), her sons fought, and she lost them both due to sin. Her loss was great.

The Bible does not end with the murder of Abel, and it also does not go into many of Eve's struggles or victories after leaving the garden. Eve is the first organic wife. She had to learn to live off the land and make everything she needed from the things around her. Luckily I was born in the 1970s…were my husband's survival dependent upon my resourcefulness, we likely wouldn't make it. Eve picks herself up and has another son. Seth is a reminder to us (and Eve) that God did not forget Eve. God sees her in her newly made clothes, serving some weird meals to her family. God sees her tears and struggles.

What is God's idea of what my life should look like? He didn't give me fig leaves and tell me to cover up my ugliness. In Jeremiah 29:11, God promises me (and you) a future and a hope.

Let's take a look at what we can learn from Eve.

1. Beauty is only skin-deep and self-talk will destroy you if you let it. We demolish arguments and every pretension that sets itself up against the knowledge of God, and we take captive **every thought** to make it obedient to Christ (2 Cor. 10:5).

2. Shame has no place in your life. Being organic and perfect is not the only way. You cannot compare yourself to the perfection displayed on social media or the mom down the street. You must be the best you that God made you to be, and if donuts are involved, even better.

3. *Sin happens!* We all make mistakes and make choices that are sinful. The best news is that God gave his only son to die on the cross to forgive those sins. Sin is not the end of the story. Eve and Adam were not killed because of their sin. God loves us enough to forgive our sins and to give us a way to not be ashamed in His presence.

Today, take time to walk in God's forgiveness and hear what he has to say about you!

You already made a list of your self-talk, now make a new column with the title "God's words." What words do you know from scripture, worship, prayers, and His still small voice that you can place next to your self-talk words? Jot those down and let God's talk shine on them.

Reflection Verses

When you pass through the waters,
    I will be with you;
and when you pass through the rivers,
    they will not sweep over you.
When you walk through the fire,
    you will not be burned;
    the flames will not set you ablaze.

Isaiah 43:2

Do not be anxious about anything, but in every situation, by prayer and petition, with thanksgiving, present your requests to God. And the peace of God, which transcends all understanding, will guard your hearts and your minds in Christ Jesus.

Philippians 4:6-7 NIV

Praise the LORD, my soul,
    and forget not all his benefits,
who forgives all your sins
    and heals all your diseases,
who redeems your life from the pit
    and crowns you with love and compassion,
who satisfies your desires with good things
    so that your youth is renewed like the eagle's.

Psalm 103:2-5

twenty-five

Unloved One

Genesis 29

We meet Leah in a field with her father's sheep, which I think tells us a lot about her future. Watching sheep was a hot, smelly, thankless, and mostly boring job. Her story is of full of disappointments and lacks people who see her as a beautiful woman of God. Yet we will see how Leah impacted generations in the midst of her loneliness and rejection.

Leah is described in the Bible as a woman with weak eyes. What does that mean? I do not pretend to fully understand. I did some research and there are several weird paths you can go down to interpret the meaning; ideas like she would have needed glasses, that she was hard to look at because of her ugliness, or even that her eyes were a window to her ugly soul.

Simply put, it likely meant she wasn't the most gorgeous or the most confident woman in the Bible. Leah is given to Jacob under the cover of night as a trick. I know the focus of the story here is

Jacob working for seven years and getting Leah instead of Rachel, yet my mind cannot get over the fact that Leah's dad thought so lowly of her that he had to trick someone into marrying her. We're not told Leah's side of the story, whether she knew it was a trick or if she thought Jacob wanted to marry her. All we really know is that she wanted to be loved, but she sadly was not wanted or loved by her father or her new husband.

She spends most of Jacob's story trying to gain his approval, but we'll join her story after she's given birth to several of her boys. Leah and her sister, Rachel, do not have a relationship we should envy. They share a husband; one is loved and childless, the other overlooked with several sons. I find it interesting how the Bible focuses on their fight for Jacob's attention throughout Genesis chapters 29 and 30.

In Genesis 30:14-24, Rachel and Leah have their first recorded fight. Leah has been given a gift of mandrakes from one of her sons. Mandrakes were used for their good scent and were thought to help with fertility. Rachel asks for some, and Leah speaks her truth: "you already have our husband, what more do you want?" Leah already had several boys, but she had a need to be wanted. She traded the mandrakes from her son to Rachel for time with Jacob. She conceived two more boys after this trade. I love that the Bible doesn't leave it to chance that her conception might be the mandrakes, Jacob, or anything that Leah may have done. It states, "God listened to Leah and she conceived." This was God's love for Leah. He saw her struggling and showed her His love in the way she needed.

We then see that she misunderstands God's love by the naming of her boy, Issachar, "God has rewarded me for giving my maidservant to my husband." Leah sees her sacrifice as so great that God needed to reward her.

Today as I was taking a walk with my 13-year-old daughter, she was sharing her struggles and joys. She shared that she felt like her struggles are not as big as everyone else's. Sometimes it can seem like no one else notices or cares. "Yes, sweetheart, many do not see others' struggles as big as their own. We must accept that there is a storm cloud in our life, yet strive to find a silver lining around it." Leah embraces the storm clouds of her life, but yet she doesn't see God's favor. In fact, she reminds me of the cartoons with a rain cloud that follows them all around town.

How often in life do we do this? We focus so hard on our current problem that we can't see the big picture. I struggle with it all the time. I spent 10 years in my marriage praying for a child and cried every month when I discovered I wasn't pregnant. Then I got pregnant and thought everything would be fixed; now my dream of having lots of children would become a reality. You know, all those ladies who struggle having their first baby and then—*poof!*—they have five kids. That was going to be me! Boy did I have big faith.

Several miscarriages and 13 years later, I am the mom of one beautiful girl. I spent years, yes I said years angry at God, not seeing the blessing he gave me. I only saw what I was denied. I only saw that I had one child, that she would be alone. I couldn't step back to see how much of a miracle it was to get the one, and for it to be her!

Take a minute to look at the struggle you're going through right now. As you look at the problem, ask God to show you the bigger picture. Ask God to show you His view. Now write it down, seeing your problem through the lens of your Father in heaven.

Leah struggled with seeing the love of the Father in her life. She felt the rejection, never seeing how many blessings she had. She was married with many sons, her family had wealth, and God had big plans for her beyond the life she lived on earth. Her son, Judah, was the head tribe from where the line of Jesus came.

We fast forward through Leah's life to the death of her sister Rachel. Rachel, the one Jacob loves, dies after giving birth to Benjamin and Leah ends up raising her sister's youngest child. The Lord saw Leah as she struggled through life. He saw the whole picture: a woman who wanted to be loved but never saw the love God gave her in each child she was given. He loved her so much he even gave her a bonus child to raise.

Leah's mothering landed her in the history books. She may not have seemed too extraordinary when written about in the Bible, but her legacy lived on through her children who changed the course of the world by becoming a new nation.

Leah is remembered for not being loved by her husband, for being the undesired wife. God saw a bigger picture and made her the mother of a nation.

We may feel like our lives are ordinary. Really, my life is ordinary. Day in and day out I cook, clean, work. I do not always see God's big picture, but I do know that He calls us to take one step at a time. God did not show Leah the big picture. He gave her one baby at a time to raise to follow Him.

What is the next step that God is asking you to take? It may be something ordinary like texting a friend after you prayed for them or sending a plate of cookies to your new favorite author (see my address below). But your small thing can be someone else's game changer.

Your next step may also be something way outside your comfort zone. I am here to say go for it! Whether it's risky or safe, take that next step. Go and find that adventure God has planned for you. See what He can do with your ordinary life!

Reflection Verse

Have I not commanded you? Be strong and courageous. Do not be frightened, and do not be dismayed, for the Lord your God is with you wherever you go.

Joshua 1:9 ESV

twenty-six

Regular Teenager

Luke 1-2

Arguably the most famous woman in world history is Mary, the mother of Jesus. Some refer to her as the mother of God, blessed virgin Mary, Saint Mary. She has thousands of statues made in her image. She is a big deal!

When you read about her in the Bible, it's easy to feel underwhelmed. Mary comes from very humble beginnings and humbly lives her life. Even through the brief three-and-a-half years of her son's ministry, she is not exalted into fame and wealth. She is most certainly not someone people of her time would have thought could be famous. There's actually very little written of her in the Bible after the birth of Jesus. So why is she so adored today?

I know, I know. She gave birth to the son of God. Please do not think I am making light of her role in history. She was a chosen vessel. But wasn't she more than the vessel God used to bring his son to the earth?

Women deal with infertility issues in many bible stories, but not Mary. Mary is a virgin who God uses to bring his son into the world. She has the exact opposite problem of most other women in the Bible. Even her cousin, Elizabeth, dealt with infertility issues and prayed for years for her unlikely pregnancy. This miracle for Mary was really something beyond her imagination. I love how God weaves these two together, giving them each an unexpected pregnancy. One as a long-awaited answer to prayer, the other as a complete shock.

Mary is young and engaged to be married. According to tradition, she was most likely a teenager when the angel visited and told her of God's plan. Since normal teenagers handle life's twists and turns so well, I give her great credit for keeping a calm head in the presence of an angel. Teenage me would have talked too much for the angel to get a word in, and to be real, I still may talk too much.

The Bible says Mary is confused or troubled by Gabriel's greeting. He says she is blessed and highly favored. What does a teenager think he means by that? "Dude, do you know who I am? You must be looking for Martha down the road, she's got it all together."

Gabriel responds before she can speak, and in his soothing angel voice tells her, "God has chosen you and you are going to be a mom of the Lord's son." (paraphrasing mine)

Okay, here is where she loses it. Right? Most teenagers are emotionally prepared for this kind of news. Sarcasm is high is that last sentence. This is where I'd start giggling uncontrollably. I laugh myself to tears in stressful moments.

Not Mary. She states her concern clearly, "I am a virgin, how can this be?" See what I mean? She is calm and logical. Me? I would have shuddered, laughed, and then asked questions like how, when, and why? Mary gets right to the point. I think this is one reason she was chosen by God. Her faith *and* her common sense. She needed to be a woman who loved God and did not get rattled easily.

Mary says, "I am the Lord's servant, may it be what you have said." Then the angel leaves.

Talk about a life-changing moment. Mary's been visited by an angel and the world as she knows it is about to change forever. Let the waiting game begin. She couldn't run to the drugstore on the corner and grab a pregnancy test. It was likely months before she knew for sure that she was with child. I think her confirmation came when she went to see her cousin Elizabeth. Elizabeth's baby jumped when Mary came! What a fun way to confirm God's plan. There's been no better birth announcement since.

What Mary does next is beautiful, and perhaps a bit unexpected. She writes a song. A song of humility and praise to God. She lifts God's name up with every verse, never once mentioning herself, but praising and thanking God for his favor on her. Wow, she was pregnant with God's son and not once did she make it about her.

I learned a thing or two from her example, namely that I tend to make everything about me. What about you? Take a minute to write down some things you have, like a job, food, or a home. Now, take just a few moments to write down some things you've accomplished. As you look at this list, large or small, note who helped you get and accomplish each of those things. I bet you'll find God's fingerprints all over each of them.

As Mary grows closer to the birth of her son, the trials continue. This miracle has come with lots of problems for her. She got pregnant out of wedlock. She had to rely on God for favor with her future husband. (Can you imagine what she expected his reaction to be?) And now they must travel across the country on a donkey. Not my idea of a fun baby shower… dirt, animals, and camping? Not my thing.

Mary must have been so tired of and from traveling. All she wanted was to set up her home, make the baby's nursery perfect. Traveling to her husband's homeland with no hotel reservations isn't exactly her ideal situation. And then she gave birth in a barn! We see Mary in the nativity scene with a halo, making it seem like labor was an easy feat for this saint. But I believe that nothing was easy about being Jesus' mom. Yes, *he* was perfect, but we all know Mary was not perfect. She would have burnt meals, worried, cried, lost her temper, and made the same mistakes we all do throughout Jesus' life.

Side note to all the moms out there: You are not raising the Savior of the world! Your child is not perfect and they will sin. They will lie and drive you to your breaking point. Give yourself grace! Mary was not a perfect mom; you do not need to be one either!

We hear very little about Mary's motherhood journey through Jesus' childhood, teens, and twenties. Her words are not denoted by a different color in the Bible. She fades from the spotlight just as quickly as she came on the scene. I can't stop thinking of how hard life must have been for her. When Jesus started his ministry, he was not popular in his hometown. Mary would have heard all the whispers. She would have been painfully aware of the inside jokes people made about him and her family. Yes, we know Jesus was the son of God, but to the community who watched him grow up, he was Joseph's son. He was a simple carpenter out causing a ruckus wherever he and his followers went.

I think Mary became a saint not because she gave birth to the son of God, but because she reared, loved, and stood behind her son no matter what others said about him. The heartbreak of losing a son is unimaginable. Losing a son because people "hate" or fear him would have been so hard to stand. To watch soldiers spit on and mock your beloved firstborn is something no mom should ever have to bear. God must have known that she would lean into her belief in Him throughout it all. Even in the midst of her immense pain, she didn't reject God.

Many of us go through trials and ask God "why." I know I do. And if I'm being real, sometimes it's even more of a *WHY?* Mary was an imperfect parent who loved her son even when she did not agree with his choices. I would have been like, "Jesus get your tail home and stop this healing stuff before they try to hurt you." She supported God's plan for her son, both his life *and* death. She may not have understood the reasons for everything that came to pass, but she trusted in God.

Mary shows us that supporting someone else's dream can be just as hard as following our own. As we finish this chapter, take some time to think about the people God is calling you to support. Their path or dream may seem crazy, maybe even dangerous. With God, anything is possible. Your support throughout their process will be crucial for them, whether they fail or succeed. And how sweet it will be to stand beside them in their victory. Just like Mary, who got to see her son in the most world-changing event: His resurrection and return to heaven.

Reflection verse

Mary responded, "I am the Lord's servant. May everything you have said about me come true." And then the angel left her.

Luke 1:38 NLT

twenty-seven

Almost a Hero

Ruth 1

No, her name is not a typo. Orpah is a little-known character in the Bible, not to be confused with the twenty-first century female media mogul. Tradition says Orpah may have been Goliath's grandmother, and though my husband warned me that she's not exactly a hero, her story is so different from many others that I couldn't leave her out. Let's see what lessons we can learn from this lady.

We meet Orpah in the book of Ruth. Her husband has died and she's been put into a situation that I'm sure none of us would envy. Her sister, Ruth, and her mother-in-law are heading back to her husband's native land. She's not familiar with this land, and the only family she'll have there is by marriage. Furthermore, tradition says that Ruth and Orpah are not only sisters, but the daughters of a Moabite King. They were royalty in their land. So Orpah's options are to stay in Moab and live like royalty, or leave for

Bethlehem with your mother-in-law, where you know no one. For many, this may not be a difficult decision, but my mother-in-law is awesome! (Really.)

Orpah decides to go to Bethlehem with Ruth and her mother-in-law, where Moabites were hated. We don't know exactly when in the story she changes her mind, but she does, and Orpah goes home to Moab, to follow their customs and serve their gods. The word "quitter" comes to mind.

All the things I read about Orpah referred to her as stubborn or double minded, but I do feel sorry for her. She was a young woman who must have been in lots of pain and very confused. She was *this close* to being part of a beautiful story of renewal and hope. But by walking away from Naomi, Orpah also walked away from God. The Bible says she went back to her people and her gods. Orpah's not mentioned again after saying good-bye to Naomi. She was almost a part of the miracle.

So was she just not loyal like Ruth? Was she scared? We may never know. Her story is one that doesn't have a happy ending. We only know through Jewish traditions what happened.

I've thought long and hard about what I might have done, and honestly, I would like to think I would've faced my fears and stuck with my mother-in-law. It would've been hard, but I think I would have said, "My God is your God." I don't think Naomi was shocked by the news of Orpah going home; I think she was shocked by the fact Ruth was staying. Our natural tendency is to go home when life gets hard.

In our world it's not easy to see the straight path. Our paths often go through a dark valley or two, and all we see are the victories of others. As I write this, I'm going through a private valley. I've just been laid off from a job I held for fifteen years; it's been our main source of income for fourteen. Those who know have said it's for the best, but I'm silently mourning a loss that I feel no one understands. I'm scared beyond what words can express. I see no path. I only feel loss. I want someone to throw me a lifeline, give me hope. I want to numb the loss and feel like I am moving forward. I might even move to another country if it would help me run away from the problem. I know in my mind that this is temporary; it's just a job. The emotion of wanting to stay and snuggle under the covers is real.

We all have losses that may seem small to others, yet they send you to your bed. It may be a struggle to get up every morning, let alone thrive in the plan God has for you. So the question is: how do we not become an Orpah? How do we keep going, trudge through our emotions and find God's plan? Loss is real. In the grand scheme of life a job loss is a blip, but here we are friends. Each valley we face is dark, until we see the light. We know the rod and staff guiding and comforting us, but sometimes we need the light to see them. Dark places are just that, until light comes to them.

Give yourself time to mourn the loss in your life. Don't just say, "God has a plan," and then ignore the rollercoaster of emotions that accompany loss. I am not an expert on loss, yet I have experienced enough of it to know that not dealing with the emotions through the lens of the promises of God will cause more damage than the original loss. God has given each of us a source of light in our valleys. In his infinite forethought, God wrote down his promises to us in the Bible. In that, he gave us examples of his provision. He gave us examples of those who messed up and he still used them anyway. He gave us hope and forgiveness by sending his son to die on a cross for us. He gave us hope that loss is not the end of our story by resurrecting his son. No matter our loss, our story is just beginning.

Orpah missed out on being part of the lineage of Jesus because she allowed her grief and fear to direct her decisions.

What are you afraid of? How would you live differently if you weren't afraid? Orpah let fear step into her situation and she only saw the negative of going forward. The unknown land, unknown people, and unknown future kept her from God.

I struggle with fear. *#thestruggleisreal*

Fear of not being perfect, fear of rejection, fear of my shadow, you name it. I deal daily with fear in many situations. My theme verse is "God did not give us the spirit of fear, but of love and of power and a sound mind" (2 Timothy 1:7). Fear is the opposite of a sound mind. And even though I know in my mind that everyone fails, and that failure can even be useful, the fear of failure has held me in bondage to relationships, jobs, fitness plans I never started, and more.

Let's write down a list of our dreams, big and small. I mean real dreams (some may call them goals). I usually avoid the word "goals" because it means I can do something about the dream. So let's call them goals!

You may have a list already, or like me, 2006's list of New Year Resolutions might be your latest list. Let's put them into several categories.

1. Physical. This is where we're going to put weight loss, fitness, sleeping, and food habits. The list could go on and on. *My goal:* Daily walks. These help my body, mind and soul.

2. Financial. Goals of where you want to be next month and in one year. *My goal:* To cut my spending at the dollar store to less than $25 a month. We may get rich if I can stick to this one.

3. Time. How can we spend our time more wisely? This goal can be both personal and professional. *My goal:* Spend less than one hour a day on my phone. Spend time chatting with those around me; look up from the phone!

4. *Growth.* In what area(s) of your life do you need to grow? We all need to continue to improve and learn. *My goal:* Write a book. A big stretch for me personally, but if you're reading this, I guess I succeeded!

5. *Dream.* What do you daydream about? Let's take steps to make it a reality. What action plan can you put into place? What's your next small step? *My dream:* TRAVEL! I love being on the road, even if I can only afford a tank of gas to drive to see the fall leaves. I need to take the small steps to make it a reality.

6. *Spiritual.* You thought I would forget this one! What are you putting into your soul? What are you watching, reading, listening to? Is it bringing peace to your life? Are you in a constant state of worry? Take a close look at what you're allowing into your heart and mind. God wants us to live in HIS peace, a peace so surreal that it doesn't make sense when you look at your situation. Peace that follows you into every situation, even the meeting with your angry, unreasonable boss! What steps do you need to take to spend more time with the God of Peace, seeking his will for you?

My goal: Memorize more scripture. I love having scripture all around the house to remind me of God's promises, now it's time to cement them into my mind and heart.

Learn from Orpah. Mourn when it is time to mourn, find God in your valleys, and step out despite your fears!

Reflection Verse

The LORD is my shepherd;
    I have all that I need.
He lets me rest in green meadows;
    he leads me beside peaceful streams.
    He renews my strength.
He guides me along right paths,
    bringing honor to his name.
Even when I walk
    through the darkest valley,
I will not be afraid,
    for you are close beside me.
Your rod and your staff
    protect and comfort me.
You prepare a feast for me
    in the presence of my enemies.
You honor me by anointing my head with oil.
    My cup overflows with blessings.
Surely your goodness and unfailing love will
      pursue me
    all the days of my life,
and I will live in the house of the LORD
    forever.

Psalm 23 NLT

twenty-eight

Great Baker

2 Kings 4:1-7

When we meet Elijah, ravens are bringing him food by a stream. He's living his best life. The Bible says the Lord dried up the stream and Elijah had to move on. His moving on happened just in time for the poor widow in Zarephath. I'm going to take the liberty to name the widow of Zarephath, Jess. I have a friend named Jess and she is the best baker I have ever known; she makes magic out of oil and flour!

Jess was outside of town gathering sticks to make her last meal for her and her son. Elijah is told by God that this woman will supply a meal for him, but God didn't let Jess in on this secret. Elijah asks Jess for something to eat after she brings him water. Just as he asked the ravens, Elijah asks Jess for bread. He has no idea that Jess is about to make her last meal.

When God tells you to ask someone for something, you would assume they have it. For Jess, this was not the case. She only had a handful of flour and a few drops of oil left. She was collecting wood to make her last meal and prepare to die. Hope was lost!

When you think all is lost, it's the best time for a miracle. Elijah may not have known his hunger would change the life of a widow and her son, but God uses the most unlikely situations to show his love and miraculous power. We all want to see God's miracles before we get down to our last handful of flour.

Sometimes miracles come before we get to our end, and other times they come when we think it's too late. God's timing is not always the same as ours. Yet, when God steps in, we know it's his perfect timing.

A random act of kindness may be the miracle someone needs. Be open to opportunities to make a small difference in someone else's life.

Jess is given a choice here: to help this man she doesn't know or to feed her child one more time. It seems like a no-brainer to me. There was no chance for crops to grow in the midst of a drought that dried up the streams. It's easy to help others when you see bounty all around you, but harder when you see empty fields and cupboards. Fear already had a grip on Jess. She saw death and devastation all around her. There was no sign of rain, which meant no hope for a future. The lack of rain for that length of time changed her life. Jess only saw hope in the release of death.

When Elijah said he was from the Lord, there was a glimmer of hope. My guess is that glimmer justified the risk to feed him her last meal. She was going to make two meals, so she would just give hers to Elijah. It was worth a shot. Death was on their doorstep.

In 2020, I was working at a school when a two-week closure was announced due to a new virus that would spread fast and kill many. The fear was high, but the bounty of our cupboards was still good. Many offered to help others during this time. Then, in my state, the closure of everything came and stayed long past the two weeks. As supplies dwindled, fear grew, and the offers of help seemed to dwindle as well.

Students never did go back to school that spring in my state, and months later we were left wondering if they would go back in the fall. The fear was growing, not getting better. Things were supposed to be back to normal after a month, and six months later, not much had changed.

The coronavirus pandemic may not be the drought of Elijah's time, but it is a small sampling of the desperation the people must have felt. My faith wavered many times. The world we knew is gone. Things may never be the same. People have died. The way we shop has changed. The way we look at life has changed. I will never take toilet paper for granted again!

Drought changed everything for Jess and those around her. Her neighbors weren't bringing over muffins to help her since she was a widow. We do not know if she lost her husband before or after the drought, we only know she is alone. No one wants to get down to a handful of flour and oil before they see a miracle. We want a miracle when the jar is half full, or even better, just send free pizza to my door every day. Even with that miracle, though, we might be like the Israelites and their manna in the desert. "We need variety, God. This is too boring."

I love that Jess does not complain to Elijah. She gives him the real facts and then brings him the bread. The next day may have been the real test. It was a fluke that the flour stretched for three people, right? When I think about how my mind works, it might have been a week before I believed it was really happening. Every day thinking, could this really work again today? Jess went from planning her last meal with her son to supplying food every day for her family and Elijah.

I've wondered if Jess ever worried about the future. What happened when the Lord brought the rain? Elijah said the miracle would continue until rain came. I know nothing about agriculture, but I do know it takes both water and time for food to grow. How weird would it be to know you only have a day's worth of food at a time. No overflow. God needed to work a miracle every day for your food. I'd sure be hoping that God didn't forget about me on a day that other people needed his attention!

We so often use God like an Amazon cart. We go to the system, let them know what we want, and expect it to be delivered in two days. Living life like Jess did takes real guts. I know dying was the alterative, but she still needed nerves of steel. Jess was fully dependent on God for her life, which could have been both exciting and scary. She leaned into God's love just to make it through the day, and trusted him to show up tomorrow. Jess was thankful to have been chosen by God to be saved, and I'm sure she knew many others who would have traded places with her in a heartbeat.

Jess shows us that full dependence on God is scary and rewarding. You may never be down to a handful of flour, but when you're facing a horrible illness? Can't find work in the middle of a global pandemic? Facing the loss of a child? Full dependence on God is what you'll need to get you through.

God will continue to supply our needs better than Amazon can, we just need to ask for his help and be willing to accept it in whatever way he sends it. God's help may be a "one cup of flour at a time" miracle, not a bakery truck delivering by the truckload to your home.

Reflection Verse

You keep him in perfect peace
 whose mind is stayed on you,
 because he trusts in you.
Trust in the LORD forever,
 for the LORD GOD is an everlasting rock.

Isaiah 26:3-4 ESV

Delight yourself in the Lord,
 and he will give you the desires of your heart.
Commit your way to the Lord;
 trust in him, and he will act.
He will bring forth your righteousness as the light,
 and your justice as the noonday.

Psalm 37:4-6 ESV

...being confident of this, that he who began a good work in you will carry it on to completion until the day of Christ Jesus.

Philippians 1:6

A Final Word

Most of my life I have lived in the shadows, hoping to make it through the day unnoticed. I have always wanted to be someone special enough for God to use. And then he put this book on my heart.

Through studying these women I saw that God loves the underdog. He loves to use those who underestimate themselves. He loves to take your broken story, make you whole again, and give you a future.

In Ruth's story we learn that taking a risk by following a path to God can result in changing generations after us. I love how we see in each of these women's stories that God has a plan for them. No matter what life throws at us, we can trust that God will not leave us. God has a place and a plan for us to make a difference, if we will just take the risk to follow Him.

When we read through the Bible, we see some of these ladies were nothing but a throw-away word, like Noah's wife. Yet God saw their significance. They not only had an impact on their generation, but most changed generations to come. Noah's wife's obedience to God saved the world. No matter how small your title, God can use you.

Rahab gives us hope of renewal. No matter what our pasts look like, God can still use us. Just like Rahab's, it may not be an easy path, and it may be full of doubt and frustration. If we hand it over to God, He will forgive us for our sins and help us to start anew.

Like Elizabeth, we can feel like we are just filling a seat at church or in life. Just a spectator, part of the crowd. But God sees you. He sees your isolation, pain, and tears. God knows all of you and loves you. You never know what your pain may lead to, but you can be sure God knows. God has a plan to use your pain for good. Elizabeth suffered by herself, only relying on God to be her support. Her son paved a way for the Messiah, what an honor she had to raise John. Life seems unfair many times. And honestly, it is unfair. But God will take our broken pieces and make a beautiful piece of art if we hand it over to Him.

It is time to find our significance in God. To seek out the redemption He has for us. Take the first step down that risky path to follow His leading. And mostly, know that God has a plan to bring you to place of hope that may impact those around you to find faith and love.

God loves you and God has a plan for your life!

Acknowledgements

A book is not finished by one person, it is finished with a team full of wonderful people.

In this journey I have had family and friends who have stood in the gap through prayer, encouragement, and long chats about these woman. I have had family who had held my hand through the struggles and rejoiced with me as I broke through.

Thank you to each one of you that have been with me on this journey.

The "Real Life with Jennie" podcast is a place where you can find laughter in real life situations along with the silver lining in the storms of life.

Subscribe or download on your favorite podcast provider, or at www.ChristConnection.cc.